Fishin' Trails

25 Short Hikes for Eastern Sierra Wild Trout

Copyright 2009 by Emerick Publishing Company
All rights reserved

Fishin' Trails: 25 Short Hikes for Eastern Sierra Wild Trout

ISBN 978-0-9788343-1-9
Library of Congress Control Number: 2009928008
Trade Paperback Edition

Published in the United States by Emerick Publishing Company

No part of this book may be reproduced or transmitted in any form for any purpose other than the individual's personal use, critical reviews or articles, without written permission from author Jared Smith or the publisher, Emerick Publishing Company.

Every effort was made to present information accurately to the best of our knowledge and based on sources believed to be reliable. The Publisher does not guarantee the accuracy or completeness of information contained herein, however, and is not responsible for errors, omissions or results experienced because of such information. Commercial services and products described or mentioned herein are provided for information and to be helpful and are not endorsed or recommended by the Publisher.

Researched and written by Jared Smith
Dust jacket, text design and illustrations by Michael D. Wheary, Calypso Concepts
Photography by Jared Smith except where otherwise noted
Cover photo of Marsh Lake by Don Gale • www.photographybydon.com

Printed in China by Everbest Printing Co., Ltd.
Pre-press production by Everbest Printing Co., Ltd.

Orders and Information:

Fishin' Trails
c/o Parchers Resort
5001 South Lake Road
Bishop, CA 93514

www.EasternSierraAngler.com • www.EmerickPub.com • www.SmithSierraPhotography.com

Fishin' Trails

25 Short Hikes for Eastern Sierra Wild Trout

By Jared Smith

Contents

Section 1: Before the Trail

Chapter 1	What's so Special about the Sierra Backcountry?	3
Chapter 2	The Sierra Trout	4
Chapter 3	Hiking: The Basics	8
Chapter 4	Tackle and Techniques	13
Chapter 5	The Most Important Chapter	18

Section 2: Bishop Creek Drainage

Chapter 1	Grass Lake	25
Chapter 2	Long Lake	27
Chapter 3	Marie Louise Lakes	29
Chapter 4	Treasure Lakes	31

Section 3: Rock Creek Drainage

Chapter 1	Mack Lake	35
Chapter 2	Marsh Lake	37
Chapter 3	Heart Lake	39
Chapter 4	Box Lake	41

Section 4: Mammoth Lakes Basin

Chapter 1	McLeod Lake	45
Chapter 2	Crystal Lake	48
Chapter 3	TJ Lake	51
Chapter 4	Arrowhead Lake	54
Chapter 5	Heart Lake	57
Chapter 6	Emerald Lake	60

Contents

Section 5: June Lake Loop

Chapter 1	**Walker Lake**	65
Chapter 2	**Parker Lake**	67

Section 6: Tioga Pass & the 20 Lakes Basin

Chapter 1	**Greenstone Lake**	73
Chapter 2	**Wasco Lake**	75
Chapter 3	**Potter Lake**	78
Chapter 4	**Cascade Lake**	80
Chapter 5	**Z Lake**	82
Chapter 6	**Shell Lake & Bennettville**	84
Chapter 7	**Fantail Lake**	88

Section 7: Virginia Lakes

Chapter 1	**Blue Lake**	93
Chapter 2	**Cooney Lake**	95

Angler's Vocabulary 98

Acknowledgements

A project like this doesn't just happen on its own. It requires the help and support of those around you and I am so fortunate to have had that support. So, with no further ado I'd like to thank some folks.

First and foremost, I thank my parents Stephen and Judy Smith for their unending support, advice, and encouragement. It was your influence which first led me into these mountains and it is because of your love of the Sierra that I was able to discover mine. Your insight at every stage of the making of this book has been priceless and is so greatly appreciated. I am very grateful to have shared the trail with you both so many times over the years and I look forward to doing so for many more years to come. I am truly blessed to have been shown the way by people with such passion and respect for the outdoors. I love you guys!!!

Thanks to my little sister Lindsey for being a tremendous source of inspiration. Even having bad knees and being smack dab in the middle of your teenage years, you still let me drag you along on some of my hikes. Your goofy big brother appreciates it more than you'll ever know. I don't think it was an accident that some the best photographs in this book were taken on our trips together, because you always bring out the best in people. I hope that we can visit some of these places again in the years to come, and find our way to some new ones too. You rock, Linds, don't ever change!!

I'd like to thank my brothers Evan and Lane for sharing the trail and sharing some shoreline with me along the way. We've seen some beautiful country and we've caught some incredible fish in the backcountry together. I'm so thankful to have two best friends that I can also call my brothers. I look forward to the years ahead as we continue exploring the Sierra backcountry in search of high country trout. Keep your boots broken in, boys!

I would like to thank my sister Lettie for doing her best to coach me on proper grammar and language. Her insight wasn't quite enough to purge the slang from my vocabulary but at least she tried her darndest! Love ya, Sis!

Even though she passed on before this book made it into print, I'd like to thank my Grandma Donna for her encouragement and example. Her humor was infectious and her passion for the outdoors was nothing less than extraordinary. I am so fortunate to have been able to spend so much time with her in the High Sierra. Her support during the first few years of this project was invaluable.

Thanks to my old friends Mike Rigney and Brent Smith for accompanying me on some of my journeys. Your company and humor on the trail are always welcome! I would also like to thank Mike for teaching me a thing or two about humility by out-fishing me on a regular basis. I realize that you must have sold your soul to the devil for the luck to do so and I'm flattered that you'd pay such a hefty price just to be able to catch more fish than me. Seriously though, thank you for all the hours you've spent pouring over topo maps with me, my friend; I greatly appreciate it!

I'd like to thank the following individuals, in no particular order…Lettie and Jason Switzer, Kevin Warner, Jennifer Sanchez, Shawn Arnold at Fish Taco Chronicles, Bob Klug, Pete Thomas, Rick and Patti Apted, Ernie Cowan, Don Gale, Steve Young, Derick & Tina, Marlon Meade, Jim Erdman at the California DFG, Jim Coats, Dave Finkelstein, Becki Drew, the folks at Rick's Sports Center in Mammoth Lakes, the Trout Fitter crew, Dave Tanksley, Ed Zieralski, Gary and Suzie Olson, Nathan Moeder, Dave Strege, Jennifer Lamas, Curtis Milliron at the California DFG, Marlo Beaman, Kathy Uptegraft, Randy and Adrienne Gylling and everyone else who offered their friendship, help, advice, assistance or words of encouragement along the way.

Thanks to the guys and gals on Fishingnetwork.net, ReelAnglers.net, BloodyDecks, Allcoast, High Sierra Topix and the Rock Creek Forum for sharing my passion for the outdoors. My experiences on the message boards have had a profound impact on my life as an angler, hiker and photographer.

Disclaimer

This book is intended to help anglers find and fish backcountry waters in areas many would consider wilderness. There are inherent risks to entering any wilderness area. The author accepts no liability for any injuries or harm, physical or financial, which may occur when visiting the places described in this book. The author is a fishing fanatic who loves to share his opinions about fishing and all things related to it. This book is full of the author's opinions about hiking, fishing, tackle and fish. The author is not a doctor, fisheries biologist, geologist or trained medic.

The elevation and hiking information in this book was compiled using data collected by the author in the field, from California Department of Fish and Game records, from USGS Topo Maps, using a TOPO Software program as well as using handheld GPS units. The data from all of these various sources did not always fall exactly in line so the author presented the material using his best judgment. While it is quite accurate, the elevation changes and hiking distances may not be exact.

Fish species distribution information was compiled over years of fishing and was in addition to data provided by the California Department of Fish and Game. While this data is the best available, it is bound to change over time. Because of this, the author makes no guarantees as to the type, size and quantity of fish found in any of the lakes covered in this book.

About the Author

Since you're about to read a book I wrote, I should probably tell you a little about myself. My name is Jared Smith and I am a bona fide fishaholic. My tendency to start salivating at the sight of any pond, lake, stream or river has no doubt cost me tens of thousands of dollars over the years. In some cases, my love of fishing and the outdoors has probably cost me a promotion or two, but looking back on my life, I don't think I'd change a single thing. The reason, of course, is that the experiences I've had while out hiking with friends or fishing with my family have had an infinitely more substantial impact on who I am and my quality of life than any promotion or pay raise ever could. It is this enthusiasm for the high country of the Sierra, and all things related to fishing, that has shaped my life into what it is today; and I am a happy man, a thankful man.

I think fishing and the Sierras are as much a part of my genetic code as my green eyes. I am the proud son of Stephen and Judy Smith, who both come from fishing families and have oodles of fishing stories from when they were kids. My grandparents also shared plenty of stories about fishing the Sierra when they were kids. For four generations my family has been enjoying the Eastern Sierra and the trout that live here. It should then be no surprise that when I made my appearance on this earth, my parents took me fishing as often as they could. As the rest of my four siblings arrived, this occurred even more frequently.

Even though I grew up in Southern California, our family fishing trips regularly took us to places like the Bishop Creek Canyon, the Mammoth Lakes Basin, Devils Postpile, Twin Lakes

Bridgeport and just about everywhere in between. My earliest memories, and to this day some of my fondest memories, are of fishing trips with my family. My Dad was our fishing guide back then. He's not an outwardly emotional man, but there was never any doubt that I was loved during those fishing trips with the family. The funny thing about those family vacations is that I really don't recall how good the fishing actually was on a lot of those trips…but the lakes, the views, the good times, and the overall experiences are simply unforgettable.

My angling experience in the Sierra started early. My first trout was caught at North Lake when I was hardly old enough to hold a rod and reel. Although I'd been carried into the backcountry dozens of time as a child, my first real memory of the Sierra backcountry is a five day excursion to the Golden Trout Wilderness when I was nine years old. In preparation for that trip, I learned how to cast a fly rod and shortly thereafter how to tie flies. My first full-on backpacking trip was to the Hilton Lakes when I was twelve. I remember hating the hike uphill but being in total awe of the destination once we arrived. At sixteen, and at the peak of my teenage angst, my father dragged me along on an 85-mile section of the John Muir Trail, a trip which exposed me to scenery so amazing that I still get teary eyed when I think about it. It was on that trip with my Dad that something clicked deep down, in my soul, if you will. I left the backcountry with a mental compass that would always point to the high country. Happiness for me would forever be in the peaks and valleys of the Sierra. From that point on, I knew exactly where to go, even if only for a day or a two, if I needed a reminder of just how good life is; and it is very good indeed.

Nowadays, I live in the Bishop Creek Canyon and manage Parchers Resort, a beautiful resort in my favorite of all places, the Eastern High Sierra. When I began work on this book, however, I was the supervisor of a call center for an IT firm in Southern California. I was living in Tustin, California but I was constantly haunted by a few short stints when I'd lived in Mammoth and June Lake in the late 1990s, a time I considered to be the best time of my life. Although I had resigned myself to my career in the corporate world, I tried to get back to the Sierra as often as I could. Thankfully, this was quite often and I was able to fish and hike frequently. Still, it wasn't enough.

Then, after a backpacking trip in August 2004, I had an epiphany of sorts and the idea for this book. What better excuse could I have to spend an excessive amount of time in the Sierra? As luck would have it, I had accrued enough vacation time to spend four days a week in the mountains for just about the entire next season. The plan was to visit, photograph, fish and document some of the backcountry lakes I'd been going to for years. The best part of the whole thing was that I would also need to visit some lakes that I hadn't seen. Thankfully, my manager supported the idea and approved all of that vacation time (I still owe her, big time!).

During the majority of 2005 my life revolved around this book. I still had to pay the bills, so every week I traveled back and forth between Irvine and Mammoth. The drive back to Southern California got more and more difficult every single week. If there was an actual disease caused by exposure to backcountry lakes, I had it. I started to feel anxiety around crowds. I found it difficult to wear anything but hiking boots. I felt a heaviness in my chest when I got too far south on highway 395. I found myself continually cursing the rat race. I even wrote songs about dropping everything in my life and moving to the mountains. I was a sick man.

Then, in September of that year, on one of my last trips of the season, I found something that changed my life and the life of my family. A real estate listing for a little resort and marina in the Bishop Creek Canyon caught my eye. Long story short, within two months I had left my job at the IT firm, said goodbye to my friends in Southern California, and relocated to Bishop, California. It all happened so fast that I had no choice but to put this book on the back burner.

Finally, after a few seasons of living and working in the Bishop Creek Canyon, I had the opportunity to finish this book. Having had time to reflect on everything that has happened, I am thankful for the extra time it took because it afforded me the opportunity to add a few lakes that I wasn't initially going to include. The extra time also gave me the opportunity to meet a host of people who have, in one way or another, affected the content of this book.

Experiencing the wild areas of the Eastern Sierra is the only way I've found to truly understand the singular beauty of it all. It is through enjoyment of these areas that appreciation is born and with it comes a kind of reverence for the world we live in. I truly hope that visiting the places discussed in this book will help to reinforce your appreciation for the Sierra backcountry.

See you on the trail!
Jared Smith

Before The Trail

Chapter One:
What is so Special about the High Sierra Backcountry?

In a word, ***everything!*** Most of the folks who read this book will have at one time or another fished for trout in a lake or stream. It may have been long ago with a family member who is no longer on this earth or it may have been with a friend sometime last week. In either case, those experiences stick with you long after the day's fishing is over.

This is even more so with backcountry fishing. Imagine that you're fishing in a place relatively untouched by man. It's pristine, beautiful, quiet and simple. Imagine having that place all to yourself. Imagine cresting a hill and being overcome with excitement as you gaze down on a sapphire-blue gem of a lake for the first time…a place that only a fraction of area visitors ever get a chance to visit and a sight that people literally travel from around the world to see.

Imagine a place where there is literally zero chance of a car alarm going off within earshot. Sounds great right? Now add to that the fact that this place is absolutely loaded with some of the feistiest and most beautifully-colored trout on earth. Now you have a mere glimpse of what backcountry fishing is all about.

But it's more than that. It's about truly getting away, if only for a few hours. It's about getting a little lost while finding yourself; it's about finding peace. It's about witnessing scenery that leaves one speechless and in total awe of the world we live in. You can feel challenged, rewarded, exhausted, excited and complete all in the same trip.

When one wanders beyond where the road ends and trail begins, that is where the magic happens. That is where the true wonder of the Sierra experience lies. It is that place where your spirit soars and your heart and soul can be recharged and renewed. It's an amazing place.

If you get nothing else out of this book, I hope you at least feel the urge to wander up to the Eastern Sierra. Feel the trail beneath your feet; hear the song of a stream as it cascades down the mountain. It can literally change your whole perspective on life; I know it has for me.

Chapter Two:
The Sierra Trout

There are several species and subspecies of trout distributed across the Sierra Nevada range in California. These following five species are the trout that inhabit the lakes covered in this book.

Rainbow Trout

When people think trout, the Rainbow Trout is what most commonly comes to mind. Over the past century these fish have been stocked in a variety of locations including remote waters deep in the backcountry and easily accessible roadside lakes and streams across the state. The difference between wild Rainbows (for our purposes we'll define wild as spending the majority of their lives in the wild) and hatchery trout, planted on a weekly basis in the local fishin' hole, is remarkable. Not only is there typically a drastic difference in the appearance of the fish, there is most certainly a difference in the fight a wild 'Bow puts up. The wild variety of Rainbow Trout is a spectacular sport fish well known for

drag peeling runs and aerial acrobatics upon being hooked. Although most of the backcountry Rainbow Trout in the Sierra are on the smaller side, they are an exceedingly beautiful and an exciting trout to catch!

Brown Trout

If trout had moods, I would describe the Brown trout as being extremely and unapologetically grumpy. Elusive, easily spooked, wary, and smart are all accurate descriptors. Brown Trout, even when found in high numbers, are caught with far less regularity than other trout species. That is not to say Brown Trout are timid fish; in fact, when it comes to their dining habits they are absolutely ferocious. For years I've heard stories about monster Browns eating or attempting to eat ducklings, chipmunks, mice and fish nearly their own size. Granted, I

haven't witnessed any of these occurrences myself but such stories are so commonplace that I tend to believe that at least some of these things must have happened. In my opinion, Brown Trout are the most difficult fish to catch in the Sierra backcountry. This is not only due to their eating habits but is also a simple matter of numbers. When a given lake has a few thousand stunted Brook Trout ready to pounce on anything that moves but only a few dozen large Brown Trout lurking in the depths, chances are you're going to catch the Brook Trout. Only three things will increase your chances of catching the Browns: Throwing larger baits meant to imitate other fish, persistence, and a bit of good old fashioned luck.

Brook Trout

Brook Trout are actually in the Char family and are not considered a true trout. Brook Trout were brought to California from the Eastern United States and are still often referred to as the Eastern Brook. In my opinion, the Brook Trout is the second most beautiful fish in the Eastern Sierra. Only Goldens compare to the brightly colored male Brookies. At their most vibrant, the Brook Trout's red belly and blue haloed red spots make for a spectacular display of beauty. Because of this, the Brook Trout is oftentimes incorrectly identified as the far less common Golden Trout. Managing a resort in the Bishop Creek Canyon for a few years has really brought into focus just how often this misidentification happens. To help you determine which is which, here are two rather easy ways to tell a Brook Trout apart from all other trout in the Sierra.

First, the Brook Trout does not have spots on its back. Instead, they have yellow squiggly lines, called vermiculations, over a dark background. The other way to tell a Brook apart from the other trout is that Brook trout always have light spots on a dark background while the other Sierra trout species have dark spots on a light background.

Brook Trout reach reproductive maturity faster than other trout and are able to spawn in conditions where other Sierra trout cannot. Combined with the fact that Brook Trout generally out-compete Goldens, Rainbows, and Cutthroats, it's easy to see why their numbers have exploded in the Sierra backcountry. There are many places  where Brook Trout have completely replaced other trout. Still, these fish are beautiful, feisty, and aggressive which make them desirable for the trout angling enthusiast.

California Golden Trout

The California Golden Trout is the most beautiful trout in the Sierra, if not the world. The coloration of the Golden Trout does vary, depending on a host of environmental and genetic factors, but the most brightly colored specimens are nothing less than nature's works  of art. Brightly colored bellies are the most distinctive attribute of the Golden Trout and their "belly orange" can range from as crimson as blood to as orange as the General Lee in the "Dukes of Hazard." There are other common traits which can help one identify a Golden. Parr marks, or dark oval markings, along the lateral line are one such trait. Little to no spotting below the lateral line and frequent large spots near the tail are a few more characteristics of these fish.

Unfortunately, most of the trout considered to be Goldens have, at least to some degree, Rainbow Trout genetics mixed in somewhere along the line. Even with some hybridization though, it is often difficult or impossible to tell with the naked eye whether you're looking at a Golden or a Golden/Rainbow hybrid. In any case, you can consider yourself fortunate to catch a Golden; they are the most treasured of all Sierra trout.

Lahontan Cutthroat Trout

Once plentiful in several California and Nevada waters, nowadays there are only a handful of places in the Eastern Sierra where one can catch these fish. Overfishing, the stocking of competing species of trout, poor water management, and dam building which prevented these trout from spawning, all contributed to their eradication from many lakes and streams. Thankfully, fisheries biologists have been able to bring them back from the brink and in some places, there are now thriving populations. Perhaps the best known Lahontan Cutthroat fishery that remains is Pyramid Lake in Nevada, but the California Department of Fish and Game does have several lakes that are managed spe-

cifically for Cutthroats. You can find some of these fish in the roadside lakes of the June Lake Loop as well as in Crowley Lake, but they are not what I would consider plentiful. The Sierra backcountry on the other hand has a few lakes which are full of Lahontan Cutthroats and nothing but. It is those destinations which I find most exciting. Cutthroats are beautiful fish often with rosy sides, large black spots and of course the bright red slashes under their jaw for which the fish were named. Next to Goldens, Cutthroats are my favorite trout to catch due to their beauty and relative rarity.

North Peak - 20 Lakes Basin

Chapter Three:
Hiking 101

Short Distance - Some Basics

    The only mandatory activity involved in fishing any of the locations detailed in this book is hiking. Hiking in and of itself is an activity that may not sound attractive to some folks but I assure you that once you've ventured past the point where the road ends and the trail begins, you'll be amazed at what you find. People quite literally come from around the globe to hike the Eastern Sierra. That goes to show just how special the wilderness areas are in the region. For the angler, breaking a sweat en route to backcountry waters filled to the brim with wild mountain trout is well worth the effort. A multitude of books have been written entirely about hiking over the years so I won't elaborate too much on its intricacies since this is primarily a fishing book. What I will do is share a few basics and helpful hints for making your day hike a safe and enjoyable one.

Knowing Your Limits

Probably the most important thing to consider when planning any backcountry excursion is your health. It is crucial that you know your own limitations before embarking on a hike in the backcountry. Not everyone is used to or ready for rigorous exercise or the thin air at higher altitudes, so I don't recommend that you take on a mountain when you're only ready for a hill. I'm not a doctor and this book is not a medical journal, so make sure you consult your physician to see if you are healthy enough for high country hiking.

> *"Know the risks, this place is wild. Always carry a map, compass, water, food, weather protection and know your health and physical limitations."*

This incredibly succinct and straightforward message comes from our friends at the U.S. Forest Service and is clearly stated on the sign at the Emerald Lake trailhead in the Mammoth Lakes Basin. The locations I share with you in this book range anywhere from 7,500 to over 10,000 feet in elevation so altitude sickness is the most common ailment to affect high country hikers. Altitude sickness usually manifests itself in the form of nausea, dizziness, shortness of breath and a pounding headache. Thankfully, a few simple behaviors can help to prevent altitude sickness for the majority of hikers.

Wildflowers can be stunning during the Sierra summer.
Photo courtesy of Don Gale

First, properly acclimate before your hike. For the average person, this means spending at least a day or two at an altitude comparable to where you'll be hiking before you engage in any rigorous physical activity. This allows your body to get used to the lower oxygen concentration in the air. Some people are more sensitive to altitude than others so you and your physician should discuss your hiking plans if you have any question as to how you'll react to the altitude.

Second, and almost as important, is proper hydration. The drier air found in high altitudes, along with other factors, makes it crucial to increase your intake of water. In my experience drinking lots of water not only helps to prevent altitude sickness but it also makes a tremendous positive impact on your stamina and in the end, the enjoyment of your hike.

The Gear

While having high dollar name brand gear won't necessarily make your hike, having the wrong gear in some instances can ruin it. Here is a list of what I consider to be the necessities to help ensure a wonderful day on the trail.

- Small first aid kit
- Comfortable daypack
- Sturdy footwear - comfortable, good ankle support and good traction are musts!
- High quality socks
- Wide brimmed hat
- Polarized sunglasses
- Sunscreen
- Plenty of water
- Snacks – a combination of protein and carbohydrates will give you quick and lasting energy on the trail.
- A Topo map of the drainage you are hiking
- Lightweight tackle box
- Fishing gear
- Camera
- Compass
- Weather protection (something warm and something waterproof)

Tell or Bring a Friend

It may seem silly, but whenever I go on a hike I always do one of the following: A. I bring a friend along with me, or B. I tell a friend or family member where I'm going and when I'll be back. Accidents do happen, folks, and there is no reason that a leisurely hike into the wilderness should end badly. Hopefully, none of us will ever have to rely on the local Search and Rescue team to get us out of trouble in the forest. Should something unexpected occur, knowing where to look and how long a hiker has been missing are absolutely critical. That information might save your hide, so make sure someone knows it!

Sierra Weather

Unpredictable is a mild description of backcountry weather. I've seen bluebird summer days start off warm only to turn windy with driving snow in a matter of hours. One of the questions I get at my family's resort is "What is the weather going to be like next weekend?" Even the official weather reports in this area often sound more like a wishy-washy horoscope than an actual prediction of weather. These weather reports are riddled with words like "maybe," "possible" and "might." It's somewhat of an inside joke between some locals that if meteorologists were clairvoyant enough to predict the Sierra weather, they'd probably be retired by now after earning a quick and substantial fortune in Vegas.

Instead of worrying about what the weather might be like, it's best to be ready for both summer heat and winter-like cold. I find crazy weather exciting and,

View of Greenstone and Saddlebag Lake from the trail to Wasco

Fishin' Trails

Wildlife is abundant on the trail

to some extent, fun. Of course that's because I'm always prepared. Preparation is the most important factor in any backcountry situation, including weather. Don't let an afternoon thunderstorm dictate the success of your high country experience.

There are two things that one should always bring on any hike: Something warm and something waterproof. You don't necessarily need to bring a heavy parka (although this can come in handy early and late in the season) but you should have something to ward off the chill. I prefer something both warm and lightweight like a fleece or fleece lined sweater. Some folks also bring along waterproof windbreakers and the like which are nice, but, for protection from rain, I typically go with the cheapie ponchos you can buy just about everywhere in the Sierra. You know the neon trash bag like ponchos that cost a whopping two bucks? They work just fine in a sudden rainstorm and in most cases, are sufficient for any of the short excursions covered in this book.

Information Stops

There is a ton of helpful, free information available out there. In my opinion, stopping at the local U.S. Forest Service Visitor Center is a must when hiking a new area. They have maps, safety tips and any special restrictions and those who staff them typically have a wealth of knowledge they're willing to share. Another place to stop is the local Chamber of Commerce and Visitors Bureau. These folks often have a more elaborate selection of books and maps available as well as suggestions on lodging, dining and entertainment for after your hike. Trust me, knowing where to get a good steak in town can be an extremely valuable piece of information after a day of backcountry fishing!

This beautiful backcountry golden was fooled by a mini-jig

Chapter Four:
Tackle and Techniques

When it comes to backcountry trout, the tackle you bring to the party is absolutely crucial. Unlike the typical planter trout you'll find in most roadside lakes and streams, wild trout aren't going to be fooled by a neon blob of goop, so leave the treble hooks and dough bait at home. In the wild, an angler's best chance of success is to use a number of artificial presentations and tactics. These techniques are, in most cases, quite simple. They not only allow for the safe release of the fish once the battle is over, but also give the angler a better chance at higher fish counts and a quality wild trout experience.

Fishin' Trails

Rod, Reel and Line

One of the most important things to consider when venturing into the backcountry, if not the most important thing, is your rod and reel setup. Due to the crystal clear waters and at times finicky nature of wild trout, ultra light tackle is, almost without exception, the best. The Sierra backcountry is no place for your ocean surf fishing gear, which, believe it or not, I have actually seen in use at Mack Lake in the Little Lakes Valley. Obviously, those folks were not catching a darn thing. The right tackle is not only important to catching fish, but if by some stroke of luck you did catch a small wild trout on 15 lb test line, how much fun could it possibly be? The answer is not much, if any.

My typical setup is a 7' 6" ultralight rod and a quality reel that holds somewhere around 250 yards of 2lb test line. Rod length is a personal preference type of thing but it should be noted that a longer rod often allows for a longer cast, a big plus in most still water situations. Of course, a rod that long does make fishing the tiny willow-lined brooks and inlet streams a little challenging, so that is something to consider. In general, your lightest trout outfit will work in the backcountry but, in my estimation, the lighter the tackle, the more fun the fight.

Hardware

Four of the deadliest backcountry lures

Just about every angler, at one time or another, has used a lure. Cast and retrieve lures are no less potent in the backcountry than they are in roadside lakes and streams. Sierra standbys such as the Panther Martin, Kastmaster, Thomas Bouyant, Mepps Spinner, Rapala and Roostertail, just to name a few, are responsible for fooling tens of thousands of trout each year and all of these lures work in the backcountry. One thing that is crucial to remember is to match the lure to your quarry. A popular saying among anglers is, "big lure, big fish" and, of course, the flip side of this is also generally true. If you decide to hike to a lake that holds only 7" to 9" Brook Trout, you may want to leave a big

Rapala plug at home in favor of a selection of small spinners and casting spoons. On the other hand, if you're fishing a lake known to contain trophy browns, bringing a plug that looks like a 7" Brook Trout may pay off big time.

While casting lures is a fairly straightforward method of fishing, a few key points will improve your success.

- First, vary your retrieve. Water temperature, time of day, season, depth and a whole host of other variables play into what entices a trout to strike. If at first you don't succeed, change it up until you find a retrieve pattern that works. Pausing or changing speeds during the retrieve will often produce fish when a constant steady retrieve isn't working.
- Lure depth can also be important, especially in deep lakes holding larger fish. Counting down a lure, or letting the lure sink for a few seconds before beginning your retrieve, can help get you into the strike zone.
- Lastly, don't simply cast straight out from shore and bring your lure in. Trout often swim tight into shore parallel with the bank so a few casts in that fashion is a good idea. Trout also like to hang on the edge of drop-offs, so casting diagonally across these areas will increase the amount of time your lure is in the target area.
- While there is some debate on the subject, I always attach my lure to a small snap swivel to prevent line twist and to make it easy to switch lures.

Plastics

Although it is not an entirely new genre of trout fishing, plastics have really come to the forefront of the trout game over the past decade. The two primary plastic baits used in trout fishing are the mini-tube jig and the plastic trout worm. Mini-tube jigs were first brought to the Eastern Sierra in the early 1980s by legendary anglers such as Marlon Meade and "Crappie John" Beale. They proved so successful that once many anglers learn to fish these baits, they rarely use anything else. The last ten years have also seen an explosion in the popularity of plastic trout worms following the release of Berkley's Power Trout worm and Lip Ripperz trout worm products. Plastic trout worms and mini-tube jigs can be incredibly productive baits for catching and releasing large numbers of trout. Surprisingly enough, even though these baits have become very popular in the roadside lakes and streams of the Eastern Sierra, I have yet to encounter anyone else using them in the backcountry. That's surprising when you consider that I tend to have more success using plastics than anything else.

There are three primary ways to fish mini-tube jigs. First, and probably the most popular, is to cast the jig to a desired structure, count the lure down and slowly retrieve while applying a slight wiggle to the rod tip. This rod movement gives a fluttering and darting action to the jig, which trout literally eat up. Another retrieve is referred to as finger jigging, which involves extending the index finger of the hand, holding the rod so that the line bounces off your finger at each revolution of the spinning reel. The other common rigging for mini-tube jigs involves fishing the jig several feet under a float or weighted bobber. In my experience, the bobber technique is most helpful in breezy conditions, when water current is a factor or when long casts are required to reach structure. With any of these tube jig techniques, a small piece of trout worm attached to the hook can motivate otherwise finicky trout to strike.

Crystal Lake Goldens Love Orange Trout Worms

While there are several different ways to rig and fish a plastic trout worm, the most popular are the split-shot rig, the casting bubble rig and the drop-shot rig.

The split shot rig is the most versatile and employs a thin wire hook on which the worm is threaded or wacky-rigged with a small split-shot sinker attached 12" to 24" above the worm.

In situations where longer casts are necessary, the casting bubble rig is perfect. A clear casting bubble completely filled with water is secured 4' to 7' above the worm and held in place with either a swivel or Carolina Keeper. In both cases, a slow retrieve is mandatory to maintain lure depth. In addition to a slow retrieve, one can employ a series of jerks, pauses or use the "finger jigging" technique as well.

Rainbows are suckers for olive wooly buggers

The drop-shot rig is perfect when you want to creep the worm along the bottom of the lake. The drop-shot is achieved by attaching a Palomar Knot to a thin wire hook and then attaching a split shot sinker to the tag end of the knot. You can vary how far the bait hovers off the bottom by adjusting the length of the tag end. I typically keep my hook 12" to 24" above the weight. The advantage of the drop-shot rig is that it leaves your sinker at the end of your line, allowing you to keep your lure a relatively consistent distance from the lake bottom. This setup is ideal for fishing steep drop-offs close to shore, a situation common at many backcountry lakes.

Fly and Bubble Combo

Probably the best way to catch wild trout is on the fly. While fishing with flies conjures up images of finely tuned experts whipping neon-colored fishing line back and forth with a fly rod, it doesn't necessarily have to be that way. For the spin fisherman, the benefits of the fly can be gained by using a casting bubble and a long leader. Dry flies, nymphs and streamers can all be used with this rig and all can be extremely productive. The clear casting bubble allows for super long casts which makes it perfect for larger bodies of water. Even in small lakes, the fly and bubble can be an unbeatable combination.

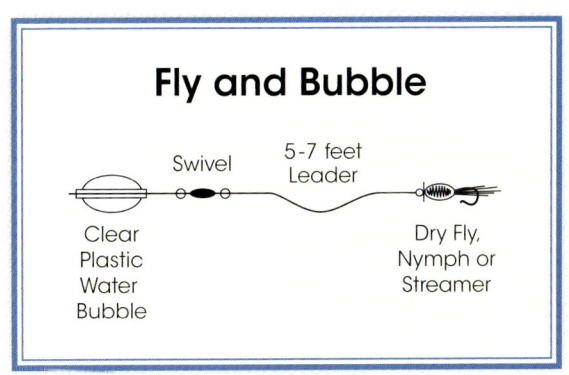

The two best choices for attaching the bubble to your line are a swivel with 5' to 7' of leader material, or using a Carolina Keeper 5' to 7' above the fly. Some of the most common flies to have in your box are the Woolly Bugger, Matuka, Sierra Bright Dot, Elk Hair Caddis, Adams, Mosquito, Blue Winged Olive, Pheasant Tail Nymph and Hare's Ear Nymph. Of course, everyone has their preferred dry, wet and streamer flies so experimentation is an excellent if not essential practice for building your own list of favorites. Typically, I use a cast and slow retrieve for most nymphs and dry flies to get the trout to play. For streamers, I count the bubble down to various depths and use more of a jerk-and-pause retrieve.

Little Lakes Valley – Upper Rock Creek

Chapter Five:
The Most Important Chapter! Outdoor Ethics

This is by far the most important chapter of this book and as such, each reader must pass a short quiz on the material in order to proceed on to later chapters. OK, that isn't true but if it was possible to do so in this medium, I would absolutely make that happen. To me, the way we treat nature's playground is a serious reflection on our character and humanity. The places covered in this book are, in most respects, examples of the perfect world, a relatively untouched, peaceful, and beautiful world decorated with epic skylines, majestic forests, and pristine lakes stuffed with wild trout. To many people, including myself, these places are sacred. It should then come as no surprise that a deep appreciation for them is what has protected them over the years. If you have any doubt in your mind as to whether or not you will be compelled to be a good steward of these gorgeous places, please put this book down and stay at home!

Litter

Some fantastic slogans have been coined over the years, some of which are often posted along the trail. "Take only pictures, leave only footprints," "Pack it in, pack it out" and the like are more than just catchy phrases; they are words that represent and encourage a respect for nature that is absolutely crucial in the high country. It should go without saying that one should not litter in the forest but, unfortunately, it still needs to be said, again and again. As anglers, we need to take this very seriously – if not only for our own enjoyment of the wilderness, then to maintain a positive image of what it means to be an angler. There is a lot more to fishing than a cooler, a lawn chair, a twelve pack of beer and a trail of litter, but far too often that is the stereotype we are stamped with. By making certain to leave the wilderness as clean or, even better, more clean than we found it, we do ourselves a big favor. Make sure that things like snack wrappers, water bottles and fishing line come back down the hill with you. To go one step further, I try to pick up any trash that I come across in the backcountry, a habit I took from my parents, having watched them do it for years. Thankfully, I usually come across very little trash in the backcountry so I always have plenty of room in my pack for a misplaced soda can or granola bar wrapper. Accidental littering is just as much an eye sore as the intentional kind so make sure that you have all of your gear and any trash thoroughly secured before you start hiking.

"That Guy"

Make no mistake about it – with the release of this book I'm basically inviting you to visit some of my favorite places on earth. That's not to say that you couldn't visit these places without reading the book, but I am, to a point, putting a lot of faith in you, the reader, when I share this information with you. Please don't make me regret that decision by being "that guy." Here are some examples of what I mean.

Fishin' Trails

- Don't be that guy who, despite being the only person other than yourself on the lake, decides to set up shop right next to you because you're catching fish.
- Don't be that guy who has a well meaning but terribly behaved dog running amuck without a leash and is oblivious to the fact that some people do not appreciate Fido sniffing their crotch or tangling up their fishing line.
- Don't be that guy who brings a boom box into the wilderness and blasts 1980s hair bands at top volume (hopefully, the knobs don't go to 11!).
- Don't be that guy who fails to understand the concept of hiking on a trail, who goes charging down the hill cutting switchbacks the whole way (I've heard these folks in particular give the trail maintenance crews night terrors).
- Lastly, don't be that guy who feels the need to carry up and finish off an 18-pack of beer and who then leaves empty cans and cigarette butts strewn about the landscape.

North Peak reflecting in a high country tarn

Look folks, people come to the mountains to relax, for peace and quiet, for solitude and for an enjoyable hiking and angling experience. They visit these places to avoid "that guy." If they wanted to hang out with that guy they wouldn't bother leaving the lakes in the big city. Don't be one of the few who ruins the experience for others.

Do enjoy yourself. Please laugh hysterically if your buddy trips over his own boots and falls in the drink. Please cheer enthusiastically when you catch your first Golden Trout, but also have consideration for others who may have hiked into the backcountry. Thankfully you'll find that the locations in this book are far less visited than roadside lakes and streams in the Eastern Sierra, but it's still important to keep common courtesy in mind, and more importantly, take it to heart.

Catch & Release

I practice catch and release 100 percent of the time when day hiking. Why? The first reason is that it's a hassle to take fish because keeping them fresh on a warm summer day while hiking through the forest is not a practical endeavor. Second, I hate cleaning fish. Those are my top two reasons for practicing catch and release.

There are, of course, a host of other reasons to practice catch and release, and many of them are valid, but there are only two other reasons I care to note here. One is that Rainbows and Goldens are becoming increasingly rare in many lakes because they are being displaced by Brook Trout. Second is that Brown Trout love to eat Brookies. The moral of this short story is that, almost without exception, releasing the Rainbows, Goldens and Browns is the right thing to do in backcountry lakes. One other thing to consider is that larger trout, regardless of species, take a very long time (think decades, not years) to grow to any size in the high altitude waters of the Sierra. So please let the big ones go, they are a rarity not often seen anymore because too many wild trout end up as dinner. CPR is the way to go – catch, photograph and release.

Brook Trout on the other hand can spawn sooner and in more varied conditions than other Sierra Trout. In most alpine lakes, this has resulted in Brook Trout becoming stunted and overpopulated. An argument could be made to take every Brook Trout you catch and chuck it over your shoulder into the woods like my dad and my dad's dad used to do with Carp once upon a time. But, this is a chapter on outdoor ethics and, seeing as that would be illegal and therefore unethical, I do not condone or encourage anyone to do that! However, if you are interested in having some trout for dinner, please keep some Brookies. You'll be doing the other Sierra trout a favor as well as yourself because Brook Trout are the tastiest trout around in my opinion. Another thing to keep in mind is that at the time of this book's release, the California Department of Fish and Game allows a bonus bag and possession limit of up to ten Brook Trout less than 10" in total length per day, in addition to the five fish daily limit for other trout. So if you have a taste for trout, by all means, do take advantage of this and load up on those little Brookies.

Now that you know when to practice catch and release, it's equally as important to know how to do it properly. It's not terribly complicated but there are few key things to remember.

Fishin' Trails

- First, always handle the fish with wet hands. The slime on the fish is what protects them from disease and parasites. Never ever use a rag or hand towel on a fish you plan on releasing – the fish may swim off fine but you may be letting go a fish that dies a few weeks later and that is a tremendous waste. Whatever you do, do not pull the trout up on shore letting it bounce around in the dirt and grass and then wipe it off with a towel or your hand.

- Keep the fish in the water as much as possible. Trout can't breathe without water so keeping them in the water will minimize the stress caused to the fish and help to ensure a safe release. If you're going to take a picture, get the camera ready while the fish is in the water and then lift the fish out of the water just long enough to snap the photo. Not only is this better for the fish but a wet glistening trout makes for a better photo!

Wild trout photograph beautifully while still in the water

- On occasion, even with artificial lures, you'll deep-hook a trout. If the hook is in the gills or gullet, never rip the hook out. In fact, don't even try to remove the hook. Simply cut the line at the mouth and let the fish swim away. In many cases the hook will dissolve or pass. Sure, you may lose your hook but it's worth a few cents to save a trout. I see people at roadside lakes "releasing" bleeding trout after using those big red hook removers on a fish that swallowed their bait. Sure, the fish may swim away but it's going to be dead within minutes. Very few things irritate me more than people releasing fish that are sure to die.

- Wild Trout are, in most cases, far heartier than their planter cousins. Still, it's important to handle these fish with care. A good net and a little patience is all you need to easily land and safely release a wild Trout. Squeezing them to get your grip is a big no-no and totally unnecessary.

Bishop Creek Canyon

Trailhead: **Lamarck Lakes Trailhead / North Lake**
Elevation: **9900 feet**
Climb: **550 feet**

Distance: **1 mile**
Lake Size: **1.87 surface acres**
Species: **Brook Trout**

Chapter One:
Grass Lake

    Grass Lake is aptly named as it lies at the edge of a huge grassy meadow. One of the shorter hikes in this book and the shortest in the Bishop Creek Canyon, getting to this small shallow lake is very easy. From where you park at North Lake, it is only one mile to the lake and with only a few hundred feet of elevation gain, it's a relatively painless mile.

Fishin' Trails

Grass Lake is simply stuffed with Brook Trout in the 4 to 6" range with just a few bigger ones mixed in. While it could probably use a few Browns to thin out the Brook Trout population, that hasn't happened yet so this lake is not a destination for the trophy trout hunter. In my estimation, that should by no means discourage anyone from visiting. I mean there are tons of small feisty Brookies in Grass Lake, which makes it a phenomenal destination for short family or solo trips where easy hiking and certain catching are top goals for the day.

One nice feature of this lake is that there is plenty of room for back-casting. The aggressive Brook Trout are eager to crash on just about any fly presented to them, which makes Grass the perfect spot for the newbie fly angler to get some practice. It's just as easy for the spin angler to catch fish and just about anything in your tackle box will work at Grass Lake. I honestly wouldn't be surprised if a short piece of tin foil twisted around a hook could make for a 20-fish day.

The feeder and outlet streams are also stuffed with beautiful little Brookies, as are the dozens of tiny canals that meander through the meadow, so don't limit yourself to just fishing the lake. You'll be doing yourself a tremendous injustice if you don't wander a bit. Oh, one more little tip: The outlet stream is a lot of fun and there is a trail that follows it quite a ways. As with the lake, it's full of Brookies!

During a trip to Grass Lake in 2007, I ran into a young couple and their boy, who was probably four years old at the time. As I sat there casting a fly and catching fish after fish I couldn't help but notice the wonderment of the young lad as he and his parents wandered the shoreline around the lake. These folks weren't there to fish, they were just there to be there, and it was clear that they were having a great time. This couple, I thought, was either very wise or very lucky having found a perfect place to introduce their youngster to the backcountry of the Sierra.

I hiked to dozens of lakes while researching this book, not counting all of the places I'd hiked to before, and I can't think of a better place to have a picnic with my family. Of course, when I have children of my own, they'll be toting kid-sized 2-weight fly rods and there will be a bit of fishing after lunch!

Photo courtesy of Stephen Smith

Trailhead: **Bishop Pass Trail / South Lake**
Elevation: **10,750 feet**
Climb: **900 feet**

Distance: **2 miles**
Lake Size: **34.66 surface acres**
Species: **Brook, Rainbow, & Brown Trout**

Chapter Two:
Long Lake

    Long Lake is the most visited lake in the Bishop Creek Basin. The picturesque landscape, the short hiking distance, and the popularity of the Bishop Pass trail as a means to access the John Muir Trail, are all reasons for its popularity. Still, among the many hikers and backpackers, there are relatively few anglers who chose to fish Long Lake. This fact baffles me because it is the only lake in the basin that holds three species of trout: Rainbow, Brook and Brown. Long Lake is also the kind of place where any angler on any given day has a chance at catching a truly mammoth backcountry trout. If you spend much time in the Bishop Creek Canyon, you're bound to hear stories, like I have, of monster Brown Trout well over the ten pound mark coming out of Long. Naturally, it's easier to find rumors of such catches than it is to find first-hand accounts. Still, I personally know folks who have caught fish to five pounds in Long Lake. It doesn't happen very often but they're there and if you're lucky enough to hook into one, hold on!

Long Lake is a somewhat unique lake in that it is long and narrow. Unlike many of the lakes in the Bishop Creek Drainage, the folks who named Long Lake didn't use much in the way of originality or imagination when naming it. Of course, the lake being long and narrow has some advantages; easy access to deeper water, for instance. Some lakes may have 20 yards of shallow water before dropping off into a bit deeper water where many fish prefer to live. With the elongated shape of Long Lake, you can cast into deep water from just about anywhere on shore.

Don't be tempted to only fish the lake where you first encounter it. The water is shallow and the fish are generally smallest here. Move up the trail and you will find many good fishing spots. About one-third of the way up the lake there is a rock bluff with cliffs going into the lake. Large fish are often sighted here. Move in with stealth because they spook easily. Then, you, too, will have your chance at a huge, high country Brown.

Even though the Browns tend to lurk in the deep, the majority of the fish in the lake are Rainbow and Brook Trout. You're more likely to hook into those at the southern end of the lake where the main inlet comes in from Spearhead Lake. A variety of lures will work but the most productive are spinners such as the Mepps Aglia or Panther Martin. The Brookies and 'Bows tend to be larger than those in many other lakes but are still on the smaller side.

Long Lake is also a great place to use the fly/bubble rig. Early in the season, say right after ice out, the fish are actively feeding near the inlets. While the summer hatches haven't started just yet, these fish will aggressively strike a fly or nymph slowly retrieved near the surface by the inlet.

For many visitors to the Bishop Creek Canyon, the short hike to Long Lake is the highlight of their trip. Once you are there, it's easy to see why.

Photo courtesy of Stephen Smith

Trailhead: **Bishop Pass Trail / South Lake**
Elevation: **10,650 feet**
Climb: **850 feet**

Distance: **1.5 miles**
Lake Size: **0.69 and 1.83 surface acres**
Species: **Brook Trout**

Chapter Three:
Marie Louise Lakes

 The Marie Louise Lakes are probably my favorite of what used to be known as the "Hidden Lakes of the Bishop Creek Basin." Although the Bishop Pass Trail out of South Lake sees its fair share of hiking traffic due to its proximity to the John Muir Trail, the Marie Louise Lakes are still somewhat hidden because they lay a ways off the main trail. The lakes were named after Marie Louise Parcher, who, with her husband W.C. Parcher, founded Parchers Camp in the 1920s. The Parcher family played a significant role in bringing trout to many of the backcountry lakes in the basin. Quiet, secluded, and undeniably gorgeous, these lakes are a must for any avid day hiker visiting the Bishop Creek Canyon.

The hike to the Marie Louise Lakes is, for the most part, a pleasant one along a scenic shaded trail. You basically hike along South Lake for the first three quarters of a mile before breaking east towards Long Lake. Another half mile down the trail there is a small wooden sign which says Marie Louise Lakes with an arrow. It is from this point on, as you descend into a long meadow, that the hiking gets good. You're not likely to see many hikers beyond the cutoff. Be advised that the deer love that meadow so always have your camera at the ready. At the end of the meadow there is a short but steep rise over which lie the lakes.

There are two separate lakes, one small and shallow, the other larger and deeper. Both lakes hold Brook Trout but the larger lake has considerably larger fish. The larger fish are harder to catch than their friends in the upper lake so it never hurts to start at the small lake to get the skunk off before trying your luck in the bigger lake. Catching Brook Trout is no big mystery but they do seem to have an affinity for nymphs at these lakes. The trusty fly/bubble rig with a flashback pheasant tail nymph gets the majority of my casts. I've never had much luck on spinners or jigs at Marie Louise but trout worms are definitely worth a try. Still, the fly/bubble combo is your best bet. Tiny dry flies are definitely worth a shot early and late in the day when there are hatches.

> "Quiet, secluded, and undeniably gorgeous, these lakes are a must for any avid day hiker visiting the Bishop Creek Canyon."

The little lake fishes pretty much the same all the way around it but the big lake does not. There are shallow weedy areas at both the inlet and outlet and while fish do hold in those areas, they are easily spooked so be tactful when making casts to them. Still, I prefer to fish nymphs and trout worms in the deeper water by making long casts towards the cliffs and working the lure slowly back to shore.

The Marie Louise Lakes are likely to be your favorite lakes in the basin once you've had a chance to get off the Bishop Pass trail and find your way to where most folks never go.

Trailhead: **Bishop Pass Trail / South Lake**
Elevation: **10,675 feet**
Climb: **1,000 feet**

Distance: **2.25 miles**
Lake Size: **12.1 and 4.8 surface acres**
Species: **Golden / Rainbow Hybrid Trout**

Chapter Four:
Treasure Lakes

    The Treasure Lakes are amazing. The distance and elevation gained to get there is the most of any set of lakes in this book but that is partly why I like them so much. When you consider the size of the lakes and the relatively few visitors they see, finding some solitude is easy at the Treasures, and solitude is just the start of it. Crystal clear water that shimmers a

Fishin' Trails

bright blue green hue in the sunshine, jagged granite peaks to the south, west, and north, and brightly colored hybrid Golden Trout all make this pair of lakes a worthwhile place to spend the day.

The hike begins at the Bishop Pass trailhead at South Lake in the Bishop Creek Canyon. Approximately three quarters of a mile in, the trail breaks off to the southwest, away from the Bishop Pass trail. It flattens out for a time, even dropping in elevation, before climbing the remaining 600 vertical feet to the lakes. I'm not going to lie to you, this is the most difficult hike in this book by quite a bit; but I assure you that it is worth the effort! You will come across the outlet stream at multiple points along the trail and I would recommend taking a break to fish at a few of these spots. The creek has a bunch of small Goldens in it and they're easy to catch. Nothing breaks up a hike like catching and releasing half a dozen Golden Trout!

When you reach the lakes, you'll no doubt want to stop to take in the view, because it is a breathtaking one. The point on the lake where the trail first finds the water is also a great place to start fishing. There are plenty of downed logs and submerged boulders around, and the hybrid Goldens are everywhere! The fish at Treasure can sometimes get lockjaw during the heat of the day but there are places where they will hit all day long, most notably at the very south end where a seasonal inlet can feed the lake well into September.

Both of the lower Treasure Lakes, also referred to as Treasure 1 and 2, have Golden Rainbow hybrid trout. The larger of the lakes holds the larger fish, which is why I spend more time fishing it. The hybrid trout are very pretty fish and at times can display markings consistent with pure Goldens. You can catch fish pretty much all the way around either lake so there isn't really a spot to avoid. I've caught these hybrid trout on a variety of plastics, spinners and flies but because the fish rarely go over 9", stick with the small stuff. If you want to make long casts, ditch the heavy spoon in favor of a fly/bubble combo or a trout worm weighted with a partially filled water bubble. The evening bite at the Treasures can be characterized as wide open and the fish go bonkers for small dry flies, or even soggy dry flies, slowly retrieved across the surface of the water. This is a super fun way to fish. It's very easy to lose track of time when you get this bite dialed in so don't forget that you still have to hike back to your car!

The Treasure Lakes were aptly named as you will no doubt treasure your time spent at this idyllic locale.

Little Lakes Valley
Upper Rock Creek

Photo courtesy of Stephen Smith

Trailhead: **Mosquito Flats / Little Lakes Valley**
Elevation: **10,400 feet**
Climb: **150 feet**

Distance: **0.75 mile**

Lake Size: **5.34 surface acres**
Species: **Brook, Brown & Rainbow Trout**

Chapter One:
Mack Lake

    Mack Lake is the first lake you'll come across when hiking up the main trail into the Little Lakes Valley. The hike is a scenic one winding alongside Upper Rock Creek. In July, there are wild flowers galore of various colors scattered about the landscape. The area is so scenic that it's not uncommon to see large groups of photographers amassing along the trail

Fishin' Trails

to capture images of the incredible Sierra beauty.

With less than 200 feet of elevation gain this hike is an easy one. There are some step-ups that can get tricky for children, or adults who aren't paying close attention to where they're stepping, but for the most part the trail is in great condition and easy on your feet. At over 10,000 feet, the air is thin up there so don't feel the slightest bit embarrassed if you get winded on your way up; most of us do. You'll see evidence of this on the hike back to your car, as you'll inevitably pass some big group of day hikers gasping at the first and only major incline of the hike. Trust me, you'll feel much better about yourself on the way down.

When you come to the fork in the trail, you're almost there; well, in some respects you actually are there, as the lake is directly to your left, 75 feet below at the bottom of a rock cliff. The easiest access to the lake is up the trail towards Morgan Pass (left), which takes you down near the inlet of Mack Lake. From the parking lot to the inlet is about three quarters of a mile.

Although small in size, the deep waters of Mack offer great fishing for wild Brook, Rainbow and Brown trout. Most of the fish in the lake are your typical 7 to 10" models but bigger fish do lurk in the depths. Because of the sheer mid-lake rock face and the reeds near the inlet, shore access is a bit limited along the eastern shore; however, there is a good stretch of bank on the inlet side of the cliffs and another stretch near the outlet. Both are good spots, but keep in mind that the majority of the fishing pressure will be in the places that are easiest to reach. The west shore of the lake has the best access to deep water and is, for the most part, very fishable.

The Browns in Mack seem to be partial to flies and red trout worms while the Brook Trout seem to prefer the orange trout worms. Small Kastmasters and Thomas Bouyants are my preference for tossing lures. The frog pattern has been a solid choice for the Browns but given the population of small Brook and Rainbow Trout, a lure that mimics those little guys is a good choice if you're targeting a trophy. These big Browns are more often spotted than caught, but they are there. In the backcountry, I'm usually content with throwing light gear for the small feisty trout and don't get too hung up on trophy hunting. Not surprisingly, the inlet and outlet can produce, although you'll need waders to get a good shot at fishing the inlet. Casting along the cliff is another strong choice.

Finding backcountry water worth fishing with less than a mile's worth of hiking is usually difficult to find. Thankfully, Mack Lake isn't!

Trailhead: **Mosquito Flats / Little Lakes Valley**
Elevation: **10,425 feet**
Climb: **175 feet**

Distance: **1 mile**
Lake Size: **4.2 surface acres**
Species: **Brook & Brown Trout**

Chapter Two:
Marsh Lake

    Marsh Lake is small and shallow but incredibly beautiful. Marsh is the second lake you'll come across while hiking up the Little Lakes Valley. You'll need to veer off the trail to the left a little ways in order to reach the shores of the lake. The view south is simply epic, a view that many professional photographers over the years have deemed worthy of capturing.

Fishin' Trails

Marsh Lake is connected to the deeper Mack Lake below and Heart Lake above. It is loaded with small Brook Trout and also holds a few larger Browns that have been spotted cruising the shallows. As is the case with most backcountry Browns, they're more often seen than caught, but the opportunity is there. I typically prefer to get lost in the scenery while tossing flies or plastics to the feisty Brook Trout, which makes for easy, almost non-stop catching. Bright colored plastics are my favorite at Marsh, especially orange and pink. I like to toss small spinners at Marsh as well, as they can be very effective.

> "I typically prefer to get lost in the scenery while tossing flies or plastics to the feisty Brook Trout, which makes for easy, almost non-stop catching."

There is a somewhat deeper pocket of water on the trail side of the lake near the cliffs that is my favorite hole on the lake. I haven't seen any Browns here but there are a massive number of Brookies hanging around. You can't always see them, especially when it's overcast, but they're there.

The deepest water is along the far side of the lake where the creek current has cut a rut in the lake bottom. This is where Mr. Brownie hides. The bank on the west side of the lake is, well, marshy (hence the name) and nearly impossible to fish. So, the best way to reach that area from shore is to cast from the north end of the lake using a water bubble. A streamer, dry, nymph or plastic worm (pretty much any light lure) will do here. Heavy lures like Kastmasters or Bouyants are a no-go at Marsh because it's so shallow you're likely to lose anything you toss.

The view of Marsh from any vantage point is spectacular. Photo Courtesy of Don Gale

Whether it's the wild trout or the photographic opportunities that bring you to Marsh Lake, you're certain to find what you're looking for.

Trailhead: **Little Lakes Valley Trail / Mosquito Flat Trailhead**
Elevation: **10,450 feet**
Climb: **200 feet**

Distance: **1.5 mile**

Lake Size: **7.21 surface acres**
Species: **Brook, Brown & Rainbow Trout**

Chapter Three:
Heart Lake

    The Little Lakes Valley Trail winds right along the shores of Heart Lake, the third lake you'll come across heading up the valley. It is roughly twice the size of Marsh Lake although its heart-like shape leads one to believe it is larger still. After passing Mack Lake on the trail, the hiking is supremely easy with very little elevation gain. That, in addition to the immeasur-

Fishin' Trails

ably good scenery, is one of the traits which makes the Little Lakes Valley so popular with day hikers. That popularity, for some reason, has not caught on with anglers.

When you first reach the lake, there is a good chance you'll forget entirely that you're there to fish. Especially on calm mornings, it really is that pretty. Eventually though, you will come to your angling senses and want to get down to the task at hand: Catching wild trout. Access along the trail side of the lake is somewhat limited by marsh grass, but there are a few spots to cast from. If you feel the need, go ahead and stop and throw a few casts, but be advised that you have yet to reach the best water on the lake.

The outlet to Heart Lake is not only gorgeous, it can also be loaded with wild trout

I like to follow the trail all the way around to where it breaks from the lake. At this point you can continue on to Box Lake or cut to your left and head toward the inlet. Even if you are headed to Box Lake above, I'd still head over to the inlet and make a few casts in Heart because there is a secondary trail starting at the inlet that will take you to Box.

The inlet at Heart is a great spot. In fact once you're there, you can have a successful fishing day without even considering a move. The fish school up at or around the inlet waiting for tasty morsels of high country forage to come rushing into the calm clear waters of the lake. With a good set of polarized sunglasses you can watch dozens of trout darting around only a few feet from the shore. Beyond the inlet, the east shoreline offers good access to the deeper parts of the lake. There are some issues with grass but for the most part you can cast over it and still manage to safely land and release trout. There are Brown Trout present in Heart, sizeable ones at that, and during the heat of the summer afternoons, they'll be in the deep water. Try heavy spoons jigged off the bottom here.

Trailhead: **Little Lakes Valley Trail / Mosquito Flat Trailhead**
Elevation: **10,500 feet**
Climb: **225 feet**

Distance: **1.75 mile**
Lake Size: **14 surface acres**
Species: **Brook, Brown & Rainbow Trout**

Chapter Four:
Box Lake

Box Lake is the fourth lake along the trail in the Little Lakes Valley. Although you can reach the lake by continuing up the trail past Heart Lake, I like to break from the trail at the far end of Heart Lake and make my way to Box via the Heart Lake inlet (after a few casts, of course). Then I work my way around the left side of the lake from the outlet.

Fishin' Trails

You can pretty much fish your way around the entire shoreline where fishing is very productive for both Rainbow and Brook Trout. Some monster Brown Trout can be found in Box, too. I have never been fortunate enough to land one of these toads but there is a healthy population of them. I will admit that it does get a little more frustrating each time I see one (which, of course, means that I not only see it, but I cast to it and it inevitably shuns my offering before slowly gliding into the deep), but the fact that I know they're there adds some mystique to fishing in the Little Lakes Valley.

Excellent shore access makes for easy fishing at Box Lake

Although flies and plastics work great at many of the other lakes in the valley, my best luck has been throwing hardware, namely Thomas Bouyants and Mepps. I'm not sure if it's an anomaly or not but the rainbow pattern of Thomas Bouyant has been the best for me. Feel free to try your personal confidence color as well, you might just get lucky.

A cast just about anywhere on the lake can produce a strike but there are a few spots on the lake which I think are notable. First, as always, are the inlets and outlet. Second, is the shallow spot about three fourths down the far shoreline. If you have your polarized sunglasses with you (which you always should have!), it will be easy to pick that spot out. The large rock outcropping is another place that is worth spending some time on and around. There is good access to deep water with relatively shallow water close by so it's no wonder that fish seem to gather there. So break from the trail and give Box a try for some great Rainbow, Brook and Brown Trout results.

Mammoth Lakes Basin

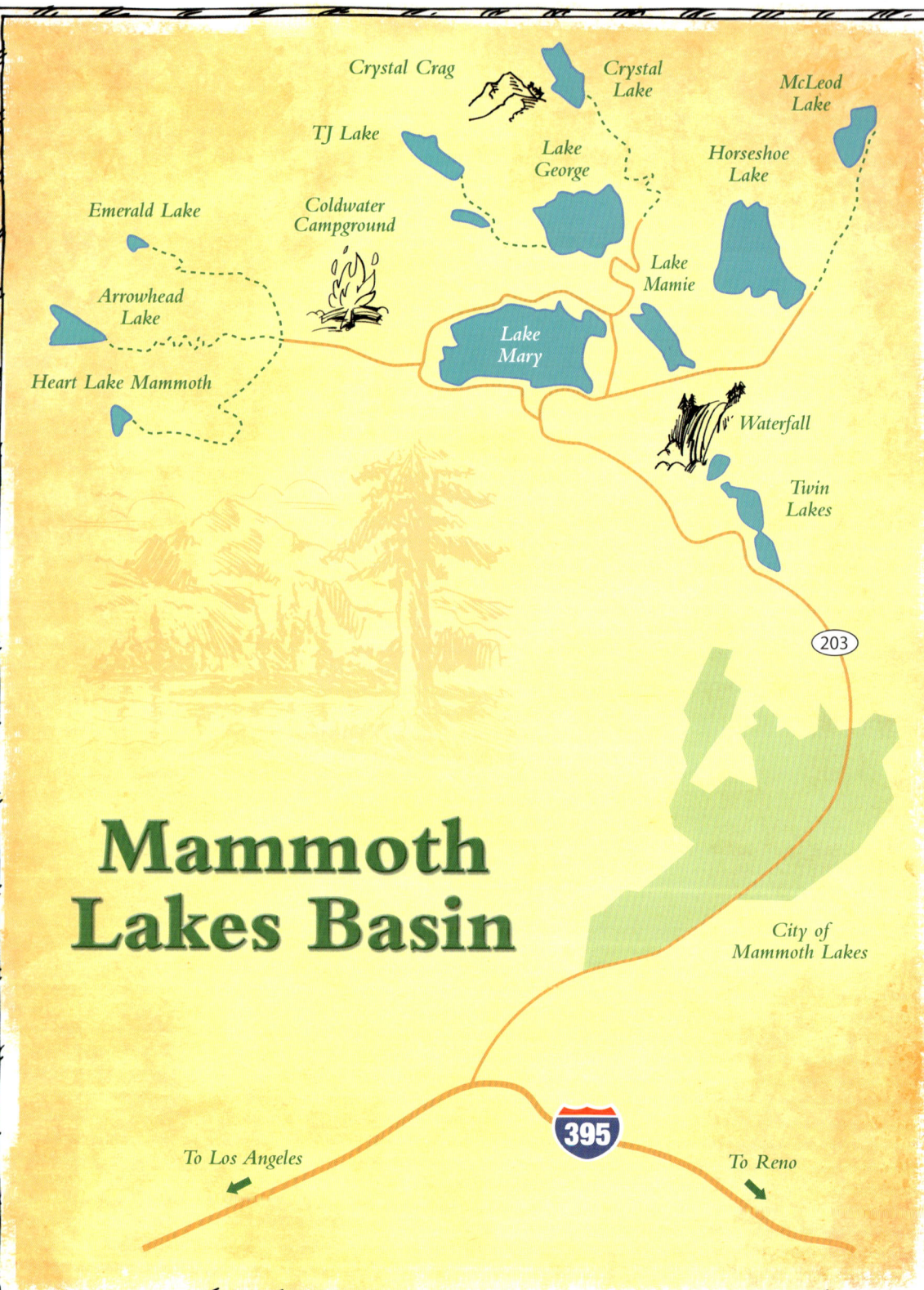

Trailhead: **Mammoth Crest Trail out of Horseshoe Lake**
Elevation: **9,250 feet**
Climb: **300 feet**

Distance: **0.50 mile**
Lake Size: **11.3 surface acres**
Species: **Lathontan Cutthroat**
Special Regulations: **Catch & Release, Artificial Lures with Barbless Hooks Only!**

Chapter One:
McLeod Lake

    At just a half mile, the hike to McLeod, also known as McCloud Lake, is ideal for those wanting a taste of the wilderness without putting forth too much effort. Most folks will make it from the barren, almost ghostly, scene at Horseshoe Lake to the clear blue waters of McLeod in fifteen to 25 minutes, even when carrying a float tube. Though the trees near the trailhead are all dead as the result of CO_2 seepage from Mammoth Mountain's volcanic roots, the forest springs back to life only a few minutes from the trailhead, making the rest of the hike a pleasant one, even on warm summer afternoons.

The most notable thing about the fishery at McLeod is that only Lahontan Cutthroat trout call this lake home, something very unique in the Eastern Sierra. Because of these special fish, McLeod is managed by the California Department of Fish and Game differently than most Sierra lakes as only artificial lures with barbless hooks may be used here and there is a zero limit. Make sure you release everything you catch at McLeod, as it is the law. The Cutties here are a bit on the finicky side so I wouldn't necessarily go to McLeod expecting a 20 or 30 fish day; but if you give it a solid effort, you're likely to connect on a few. The fish typically range between 8" and 11" with a few going larger than that.

Mcleod is one of the few backcountry lakes that is close enough to allow one to bring a float tube with minimal effort.

There is excellent shore access almost the entire way around the lake but the best bet for shore angling is along the north shore and around the inlet where you can easily access the deeper water where these fish seem to feed most actively. You'll see fish cruising near shore but, in my experience, they're not the fish that tend to bite. The south shore does offer good water if you're using a casting bubble rig because there is a shallow shelf that extends well out from shore before dropping off to deeper water. Fishing with jigs or lures isn't going to do you much good without waders at this point. Early in the season it can get tricky to access the south side of the lake by crossing the outlet so you're better served walking around the lake if you wish to fish the far shoreline. McLeod is ideal for float tubers, so if you own one and can muster up the strength to haul it up the hill, you'll likely be rewarded for your effort.

When it comes to what to use here I have to give the nod to flies. Fly anglers have out-fished me just about every time I've been here and the way I figure it, if you can't beat 'em, join 'em. Now does this mean you have to invest in a fly rod and reel to catch fish at this lake? Absolutely not! Fly and a Bubble will work here but I want to stress that long leaders and small bubbles will increase your chances. Flashback pheasant tails and hares' ears seem to produce best but you should be prepared with the usual assortment of dries and streamers as well.

For folks who prefer pitching lures, this lake may not be for you. I have yet to catch a single fish or even get bit on a lure at McLeod. That's not to say that it's impossible to catch these fish on the hardware, but I've tried plenty of times without any success. Plastics on the other hand can produce fish here. For anglers who prefer to fish plastics, stick with small jigs, preferably 1/64-ounce tube jigs, and make sure to bring at least a few different colors. Keep in mind, folks, that according to the California DFG's definition of an artificial lure, most of the popular, commercially produced trout worms are illegal to use at this lake because they are scented baits. Hand-poured trout worms are allowed provided no scent is used to sweeten the deal.

The view towards the Mammoth Crest is breathtaking

The relative scarcity of the Lahontan Cutthroat trout in the Eastern Sierra makes McLeod a special place to fish. You may not catch dozens of trout at McLeod, but the fish you do catch will be treasured!

Trailhead: **Lake George**
Elevation: **9,640 feet**
Climb: **600 feet**

Distance: **1.25 miles**
Lake Size: **12.15 surface acres**
Species: **Golden Trout**

Chapter Two:
Crystal Lake

    The hike to Crystal Lake begins at Lake George in the Mammoth Lakes Basin and is well marked. Most hikers will be huffing and puffing by the time they reach the top of this climb but don't be discouraged, even a slow-paced hiker like me can make it in under an hour – including breaks to catch your breath or to take advantage of an incredible photo-op from the trail.

The trail winds along the northwestern shores of Lake George and as you climb, the scenery gets better and better. Particularly scenic are a few unobstructed vistas that offer awe inspiring views of not only Lake George below but of Lake Mary, the Sherwins

Coloration can vary considerably between golden trout, even in the same lake

and on up towards Duck Pass. You reach the top of your climb about a quarter mile short of the lake before the trail descends a few hundred feet to the outlet stream and then on to the lake shore. When you reach this lake for the first time, you're sure to be impressed by the beauty it has to offer. On calm mornings the reflection of the surrounding peaks and Crystal Crag on the water is simply stunning!

Crystal Lake is a very special place and, not surprisingly, holds some very special trout, the Golden Trout. Aptly named, these spectacular fish call this lake home and I'm so very glad they do. Only a handful of waters on the eastern slope of the Sierra provide such easy access to these fabulously decorated fish.

For the most part, Crystal Lake offers easy access from shore which is great news for us. When I fish this lake I typically start up the right side of

On occasion golden trout take on a dull appearance

Fishin' Trails

the lake and fish to the cliffs. Then I'll backtrack, cross the outlet and make my way around to the far side of the lake and fish all the way up to the inlet. One of these days, I'll bring some waders and make my way out to the small island but as of yet, I haven't bothered. You'll find fish cruising all the way up the far shoreline and if you can make it to the inlets you'll find tons of 6" to 9" Goldens. These fish seem to hang near the mouths of the two inlets and also along the drop-off which sits about 25 feet offshore. Shore access along the western shore where the inlets come in is great mid-to-late in the season, but a bit boggy and "skeeter" infested early on.

> **"Crystal Lake is a very special place and, not surprisingly, holds some very special trout, the Golden Trout.**
> **Aptly named, these spectacular fish call this lake home and I'm so very glad they do."**

On any trip to Crystal your arsenal should include a few small spinners, some tube jigs, and flies. Fly anglers should be prepared with the usual assortment of nymphs and dries, maybe a few streamers. I've never found the fish at Crystal to be too picky when it comes to flies, but they are very picky when it comes to jigs and trout worms. You could sit there all day without a bite if you're fishing the wrong color plastic; but catch five fish in as many casts if you find the right one. The hot jig and trout worm colors change from trip to trip but if you had to take only one color, take orange trout worms and white tube jigs. Fishing these plastic baits about six feet under a bobber near the inlet is almost sure to produce a few beautiful Golden Trout.

Trailhead: **TJ Lake / Lake George**
Elevation: **9,260 feet**
Climb: **250 feet**

Distance: **0.75 miles**
Lake Size: **10.85 surface acres**
Species: **Rainbow Trout**

Chapter Three:
TJ Lake

    The trip to TJ Lake is a short one that begins winding along the eastern shore of Lake George. Once you reach the back of Lake George you'll begin the short yet steep climb up the ridge. The trail can be a bit treacherous here, so, to avoid an early end to your day, watch your step when climbing over rocks and exposed tree roots.

Fishin' Trails

About two thirds of the way to TJ, you'll come across Lake Barrett. Don't bother breaking out the fishing gear just yet as this lake is barren, but it's probably worth grabbing the camera out of your backpack. On calm mornings early in the season, Barrett offers some spectacular photographic opportunities when glassy calm waters reflect the snow covered peaks of Mammoth Crest in the distance. It's really quite breathtaking.

After taking a little break at Barrett, you'll continue along to the right and, after just a few short minutes, you'll find yourself peering down on TJ Lake. The hike typically takes between fifteen and 25 minutes, depending on how fast you choose to go.

Beautiful Barrett Lake on the way to TJ

With Crystal Crag towering above and trout often breaking the surface throughout the day, just sitting on the shores of this lake makes the trip worthwhile. The trail meets the shore near the outlet of the lake but I wouldn't start fishing there. You'll want to continue on to your left and start fishing about halfway down the shoreline, when you come to the first of the many seasonal inlets. The rocky ledges and boulders near this spot offer great access to deep water. After fishing here, work your way down shoreline, making sure to stop at the various seasonal inlets for at least a few casts. Big winters will keep many of these inlets flowing well into August, while you may only see a trickle past June in short weak winters. The south end of the lake seems to have a large concentration of fish due to the multitude of small inlets that come in here, but in order to access this stretch of shore, you'll need to leave the lakeside trail and make your way up and over a large rock formation. Make sure to fish either side of these boulders, as the water is nice and deep.

Wind around to the end of the lake to a shallow area packed with fish early in the season. You'll find the largest inlets into the lake on the far side. It can be pretty boggy over there early in the season, but later in the year, as the water level drops a bit, you'll find that the shallow shelf becomes a sandy beach which happens to be a great spot.

The Rainbow Trout in TJ can be a bit on the temperamental side, and that's unexpected given the relatively limited fishing pressure it gets. You're likely to see a few hikers while at TJ but not too many fishermen; so it goes at many of the lakes in the Mammoth basin. While I have tossed just about everything in the tackle box, or tackle backpack, rather, at these fish, the only consistent producer for me has been a gold size 0 Mepps spinner. I'm not certain why these fish don't aggressively attack trout worms or jigs like they're supposed to, but I haven't seen it. As part of researching this book, I was not only intent on finding what worked, but also what didn't work. I recall a mid-July trip in 2005 when I threw everything in the arsenal at those fish while my Dad stuck with his trusty gold Mepps spinner all morning. In addition to missing a

With Crystal Crag towering above and trout often breaking the surface throughout the day, just sitting on the shores of this lake makes the trip worthwhile.

few, he ended up landing seven spunky Rainbows while I got the skunk. Now, I'm not going to sit here and tell you that if you want to catch fish at this lake you must use spinners. By all means, experiment. But I certainly wouldn't hit the trail to TJ without a few gold Mepps or Panther Martins in my pack.

So, for backcountry rainbows in the Mammoth Lakes Basin, TJ Lake is by far your best bet!

Trailhead: **Duck Pass / Coldwater Campground**
Elevation: **9,660 feet**
Climb: **550 feet**

Distance: **1.2 miles**
Lake Size: **7.5 surface acres**

Species: **Brook Trout, Rainbow Trout**

Chapter Four:
Arrowhead Lake

    By far the most heavily used trail in the Mammoth Lakes basin is the Duck Pass trail. The trail is in good condition for the most part, and it is well defined, wide and free from debris. A well maintained trail is good news for hikers who possess an almost uncanny propensity to get lost in the scenery, like myself. Granted, sometimes getting a bit lost is part of the fun;

but in this case, even the most distracted hiker should have no problem staying on the path. The trail is primarily switchbacks until you near the top of the ridge where it straightens out above Arrowhead's outlet.

Within the context of this book, Arrowhead feels like a strenuous hike. This is probably due to the switchbacks which start at the beginning of the hike and don't really stop until you're almost there. Still, at just under 600 feet of elevation gain, it's within reach of just about everybody.

The beautiful thing about the hike to Arrowhead is that it's almost entirely through the forest. This means the majority of the trail is shaded, allowing for a comfortable mid-day or afternoon trip. You will be amazed at how much more pleasant hiking can be when you are cool.

Just as you near the top of the incline and the main trail begins to flatten out, there is a small foot path that veers off to your left and takes you down to the creek. There are a few fishable pools below the lake so taking this trail can be a fun detour. This creek-side trail takes you all the way up to the outlet of Arrowhead and eventually joins the primary trail that meanders along the shore of the lake. The main Duck Pass trail actually takes you above the lake. In fact, if it weren't for the sign denoting Arrowhead Lake you might miss it altogether. That's another reason why I prefer to take the creek detour because it not only provides you the opportunity to fish a few pools before the outlet, but it will also save you a few vertical feet of climb.

Arrowhead Lake is one of the more popular day hike lakes in the Mammoth Lakes Basin. I suspect this has more to do with the popularity of the Duck Pass trail than it does with the lake itself but still, Arrowhead offers beautiful vistas and stellar fishing for feisty Brook Trout in the 7 to 9" range and the occasional wild Rainbow as well. Brightly colored and occasionally acrobatic, the fish at Arrowhead can be taken on a variety of lures, flies and plastics.

The vast majority of the fishing pressure at Arrowhead is concentrated at the inlet or thereabouts but that certainly isn't the only good spot on the lake. Whether you fish the inlet, the outlet, the east shore or the west shore, it really doesn't matter all that much because the fish are pretty well distributed throughout the lake. I like to concentrate my efforts starting about half of the way down the western shore and then work my way towards the outlet. From there, I fish around to the far side of the lake all the way up to where the willows begin to get too thick to continue. This is all very productive territory and far less visited than the inlet area.

Trout worms in orange or chartreuse prove especially productive here. Brightly colored jigs will produce similar results especially in the shallow area near the outlet. Typically, plastics and flies are more productive than lures on the smaller model Sierra Brook Trout, but don't be afraid to cast a spinner here, as the fish in Arrowhead seem to like 'em just fine. Gold Mepps, Panther Martins or even small Super Dupers and Kastmasters all work well.

My favorite spot on this lake happens to be on the far side of the lake about 100 yards up from the outlet. Getting to the far side of the lake is easier said than done but it is possible if you're surefooted and not afraid to get a little wet should you fall in the creek. One might assume that the best place to cross is at the outlet of the lake but I wouldn't recommend trying to walk across the logjam; it is way too sketchy. Instead, I'd recommend crossing the creek a few dozen yards below the lake. There are some narrow, shallow spots where one can make a relatively easy crossing.

> "My favorite spot on this lake happens to be on the far side of the lake about 100 yards up from the outlet."

It's especially important to know your own limitations when attempting to cross water like this. For instance, if you know that you have terrible balance, hopping from rock to rock across a creek is a bad idea. Use common sense and always be careful! If you do choose to fish the other side of the lake, resist the urge to hike along the shore starting at the outlet of the lake as the willows prevent one from making effective casts and the shale is a pain in the butt to walk on. Instead, climb over the small rise. Once you're at the top, you'll see why this is a better approach as the little gulch on the other side makes for a much more pleasant walk to where the shoreline becomes fishable.

Once you reach this area you'll notice that there is a shallow shelf that goes well out from shore before dropping off to deeper water. The fallen logs submerged here complement the fact that most folks don't bother making it over to that side of the lake, and the result is that it's usually thick with fish. Tossing a trout worm, jig or fly in this area is almost sure to produce some fish.

Trailhead: **Heart Lake Trail/ Coldwater Campground**
Elevation: **9,590 feet**
Climb: **500 feet**

Distance: **1 mile**

Lake Size: **3.08 surface acres**
Species: **Brook Trout, Rainbow Trout**

Chapter Five:
Heart Lake

It's safe to say that 90 percent of the day-hikers who visit the Mammoth Lakes basin never make their way to Heart Lake. Although about the same elevation gain and distance as Arrowhead Lake, most anglers and hikers make their way up the Duck Pass trail leaving Heart Lake relatively unfished. Considerably less hiking and fishing pressure translates into

Fishin' Trails

a level of solitude that surpasses most of the basin's hike-in fisheries. Obviously, this is great news for anglers looking to score plenty of wild trout and enjoy some peace and quiet in the process.

You'll begin your hike only a hundred yards or so from the Duck Pass trailhead at the parking area above Coldwater campground. The first quarter of the hike is through the forest with the sweet song of the creek rushing down towards Lake Mary nearby. Before too long you'll find yourself exposed to the warm Sierra sun as you hike among sagebrush. Because so much of the trail is exposed, I try and stick with morning or evening hikes to avoid roasting during the summer months. As the trail crisscrosses up the mountain you'll come across ruins of old mining equipment and dwellings. I find these sights fascinating and I'm sure you will as well. The trail flattens out for the last quarter mile offering an easy approach to the lake.

> "Like so many Sierra lakes, Heart Lake is no doubt named for its shape. It offers spectacular scenery and excellent fishing for wild Brook Trout with a few Rainbows mixed in."

Like so many Sierra lakes, Heart Lake is no doubt named for its shape. It offers spectacular scenery and excellent fishing for wild Brook Trout with a few Rainbows mixed in. There is a well-defined trail all the way around the lake and I recommend making use of all of it as you'll likely catch fish from just about any position on the lake. Heart is very shallow where the trail first finds the lake so I typically circle around to the left and start casting where the water begins to drop off. Watch your step along the east side of the lake because loose rocks can be an issue if you're not careful. There is beautiful deep water here; don't pass it up.

As far as productive techniques go, in my opinion, this lake is all about jigs. Worked oh so slowly in the deep water, a bit faster and erratically across stumps and shallows, tube jigs absolutely rule. Not everyone is terribly proficient with jigs but if you're looking for a place to get some practice while still managing a few bendos in the process, Heart is a great place for you. The "hot color" varies, but oranges, yellows and reds have been the most consistent for me. For those looking to get a little edge with their jig fishing, the Berkley 1.5" power tubes in orange/yellow with a 1/32oz jig head are sure to get it done here.

Trout worm enthusiasts will find great action in the submerged stumps on the south side of the lake. As with the jigs, bright colors seem to be most productive at Heart. You'll want to use a faster retrieve in the heavy cover areas than you would while working deep water. One thing is likely though, shallow or deep: If you get the bait close to one of these trout, they're almost certain to pounce on it.

When you're fishing the shallow areas riddled with the remains of trees, don't be discouraged if you don't see any fish. Watch your bait closely while retrieving and if you see it disappear, even for a second, set the hook! Although it's hard to imagine that these brightly colored little devils can blend into their surroundings, I assure you that at Heart Lake, you'll catch the Brookies you don't see more often than the ones you do.

A beautiful Heart Lake Brook Trout

Last to be noted but certainly not least: Any trip to Heart Lake must include a quick walk to the rise above the western shore. There is a flat spot, a table of sorts, at the top of the hill, and the view of Ritter, Banner and the Minarets with Lake Mary in the foreground is not to be missed under any circumstances!

Fewer people, plenty of fish and incredible views—Heart Lake Mammoth has you covered!

Trailhead: **Emerald Lake Trail / Coldwater Campground**

Elevation: **9,440 feet**

Climb: **370 feet**

Distance: **1 mile**

Lake Size: **2.5 surface acres**

Species: **Brook Trout**

Chapter Six:
Emerald Lake

The short hike to Emerald is a delightful one. You begin gaining elevation almost immediately but the dense forest makes the climb a pleasant one, even into the afternoon. Although somewhat steep for the first third of the way, the majority of the trail is relatively flat, mild hiking and hikers of all skill levels will enjoy it.

Another bonus of this hike is that much of the trail winds along the creek. I'm not sure about you but whenever there's running water near the trail I can't help but be entertained as I peer down into the crystal clear waters searching for fishable pools and the trout that hide in them. If you do find yourself being tempted beyond your ability to resist, as I often am, fishing the creek can be rewarding and, believe it or not, the Brookies inhabiting the creek can be larger than those found in the lake.

At one point a foot path breaks away from the main trail to follow the creek up near a meadow just down from the outlet. Although heavy cover can make fishing difficult, it is absolutely worth your effort. Be advised that this trail does not continue up to the lake. Rather, it dead ends at a huge boulder field just below the lake. If you do decide to fish your way up the creek, you're better off backtracking to the main trail before continuing on to Emerald instead of trying to climb across the labyrinth of boulders.

The lush landscape surrounding Emerald is perfect for various types of wildflowers

Truly, Emerald Lake is a gem for day-hiking anglers. Aptly named, this small shallow lake sparkles in the sun with a deep green glow, attributed to the mossy growth on the bottom of the lake. Shore access is quite limited due to numerous willows and, especially early in the season, a very boggy inlet overgrown with tall grass. There are a few tight spots along the north shore, to the right of where the trail joins the lake, where one can make a few productive casts. Still, the best access is along the southwest side of the lake directly

Fishin' Trails

> "Truly, Emerald Lake is a gem for day-hiking anglers. Aptly named, this small shallow lake sparkles in the sun with a deep green glow, attributed to the mossy growth on the bottom of the lake."

across from where you first come up to the shore. You would be well served to hike around the inlet side of the lake, to make your way to the best shoreline. Not only will this route be much faster, but much safer as well. I made the mistake of climbing across the boulders near the outlet one time, a mistake I don't plan on repeating. Brimming with Brook Trout, mostly in the 5 to 9" range, this lake is a fly/bubble aficionado's dream. Because of the limited shore access, the fly/bubble rig offers a chance to reach the most water with what little shoreline you have to work with. My best success has been with a Flashback Pheasant Tail nymph. In fact, I have fished Emerald Lake without changing flies a single time. Granted, the poor size 20 nymph was virtually unrecognizable after more than 30 wild Brook Trout had exploded on the poor thing. Elk hair caddis, Adams, mosquitoes and the like will all make for an exciting fishing experience at this place, so don't be afraid to mix it up. You can cast in just about any direction and get bit but you may want to start out casting towards the little drop-off near the inlet as that spot is especially loaded with fish.

For those who prefer to toss plastics or pitch lures, you're bound to connect on

Small but feisty brookies are easily fooled by nymphs at Emerald

plenty of Brookies as well, so don't think twice about bringing a selection of trout worms, jigs and spinners. No matter what you use, you're bound to catch more than a few orange-bellied beauties if you take the time to visit this little jewel of a lake.

June Lake Loop

Trailhead: **Walker Lake Trailhead off Hwy 158/June Lake Loop**

Elevation: **8,000 feet**

Climb: **600 feet**

Distance: **1 mile**

Lake Size: **81.44 surface acres**

Species: **Rainbow, Brown & Brook Trout**

Chapter One:
Walker Lake

    Walker Lake is a most unique location. The lake is what you'd expect from most backcountry lakes, beautiful, secluded and full of trout. What sets it apart from the norm is that one end of the lake is privately owned and the DFG is able to use the private access road to stock Rainbow Trout. So, this is the only hike-in lake which is actually stocked with pan-

Fishin' Trails

sized Rainbow Ttrout. The good thing about this is that not only are there wild Rainbows, Browns and Brook Trout to catch, but a limit of stocker Rainbows is also available. Aside from these stocked Rainbows being fun to catch, they also make for very well fed Brown Trout and Walker Lake holds plenty of them. The DFG has no record of Brook Trout inhabiting the lake but I have seen Brook Trout to 15" caught right in front of me, so Brookies are there and they're very healthy!

The trailhead for Walker Lake, as is the case with Parker Lake, is just north of Grant Lake. After traveling north on Aqueduct Rd (1N17) turn west on 1S23. The lake is a short but steep one mile from the trailhead. The hike to Walker Lake is the easy part, with the return trip being a doosey for such a short hike. Still though, the beautiful setting and extremely good fishing make it a must when exploring the June Lake Loop. It should be noted that the scenery surrounding Walker Lake and Bloody Canyon above is nothing short of magnificent. Early in the morning the stillness of the lake can present one of those perfect mirror-like images of the sky reflecting off the surface of the lake with only the small rings caused by rising trout breaking up the symmetry. I love that, and I'm sure you will too.

For the shore angler, one of the great things about Walker is that there is plenty of shoreline to fish. It's also easy to reach both shallow and deep water so wherever the fish are holding, you should be able to cast to them. The south shore where the trail first gets near to the lake, is excellent deep water fishing for Rainbows. Fly/bubble and spoons have proved dynamite here. Plastics also are an absolute must at Walker, especially orange and pink. Not only are you likely to hook a bunch of Rainbows in the 11 to 13" range, but you'll have a good chance of catching a few Browns to two pounds on these as well. The shallower water is near the reeds by the inlet. I haven't seen as many 'Bows here as I have Brook and Brown Trout though, so if that is what you're targeting, as I often am, you'll want to thoroughly work that area.

The shoreline on the far side of the lake can be reached by heading towards the east end of the lake and across the inlet of the lake. While it is certainly worth a trip to the far side of the lake, I would recommend keeping those adventures to the early spring and fall; the area above the inlet can get so thick with mosquitoes that it often feels as though one is in very real danger of being carried away by them.

The unique backcountry mix of stocked Rainbows, chunky Brookies and monster Browns makes Walker Lake an absolute must when visiting the June Lake Loop.

Trailhead: **Parker Lake Trailhead - June Lake Loop**
Elevation: **8,300 feet**
Climb: **400 feet**

Distance: **1.8 miles**
Lake Size: **21.75 surface acres**

Species: **Brook Trout, Brown Trout**

Chapter Two:
Parker Lake

    Arguably the most beautiful lake in this book, Parker is also one of the most accessible. An easy meandering 1.8 mile hike and you're there. Parker is only at about 8,300 feet in elevation and considering much of the hike is through sagebrush, you'll want to hit the trail early to avoid the summer heat. You can reach the trailhead by turning west onto Parker

Fishin' Trails

Lake Road just north of Grant Lake on Highway 158, also known as the June Lake Loop. The trailhead sits two miles west on Parker Lake Road. Even though the trail is out in the open for much of the hike, there is an amazing aspen grove that, come October, is simply breathtaking. The last half mile is also gorgeous and often shaded.

Let me forewarn you that Parker Lake is not a place where one should expect to have a 20 or 30-fish day. If you hike there aspiring to catch and release small easy-to-fool Brook Trout all day, you'll be seriously disappointed. In fact, I can't say that I've caught more than a handful of fish any given day here, and I've been skunked as many times as not, but the quality of the fish is outstanding. Parker Lake is a special place because the fish that reside here are considerably larger than you'll find in the vast majority of backcountry lakes. I've caught both Brown and Brook Trout at Parker and even the Brookies can weigh a pound or better. This lake isn't necessarily a secret, as it has been mentioned in other books before, but in my opinion, any collection of easy to access hike-in lakes just isn't complete without Parker.

Stephen Smith with a healthy Parker Lake Brown

The most productive water on the lake are the north shore and the far side of the lake near the various inlets. You can catch fish anywhere on the lake but the easiest access to the deeper water is along these sections, especially near the inlets. Navigating the shore on the inlet side of the lake involves a bit of bushwhacking and I've managed to amass quite a few scratches and cuts making my way through the willows. As always, use caution.

So how does one fish Parker and plan to be successful? First and foremost, plan to spend some time at Parker. This is a lake where persistence pays off so if at first you don't succeed, try again. One should come equipped with spoons and large spinners in a variety of sizes and colors but make sure you have some large sizes so you can cast a country mile. My favorite lures at Parker are Kastmasters and Thomas Bouyants. The other rig you need to bring is for trout worms, but you'll want to forego the 3/0 size split-shots and go with

Photo courtesy of Kevin Warner

something much heavier to allow for longer casts. Whichever rig you decide to go with, long casts and a varied retrieve are the keys. If you fish Parker enough, sooner or later you'll hook up on one of the nicest backcountry Brookies or Brownies you'll likely ever catch on such a short hike. Secondly, this is one of those places where getting to the lake early really increases your chances of a productive fishing day, so plan on getting to the water as early in the day as you possibly can. Lastly, this lake fishes best early and late in the season so keep that in mind when planning your trip.

If it is the possibility of catching a trophy backcountry trout that you seek, Parker is as good a place as any. Bear in mind though that whether you catch one trout or a dozen, visiting this lake is still worth your while.

Tioga Pass and the 20 Lakes Basin

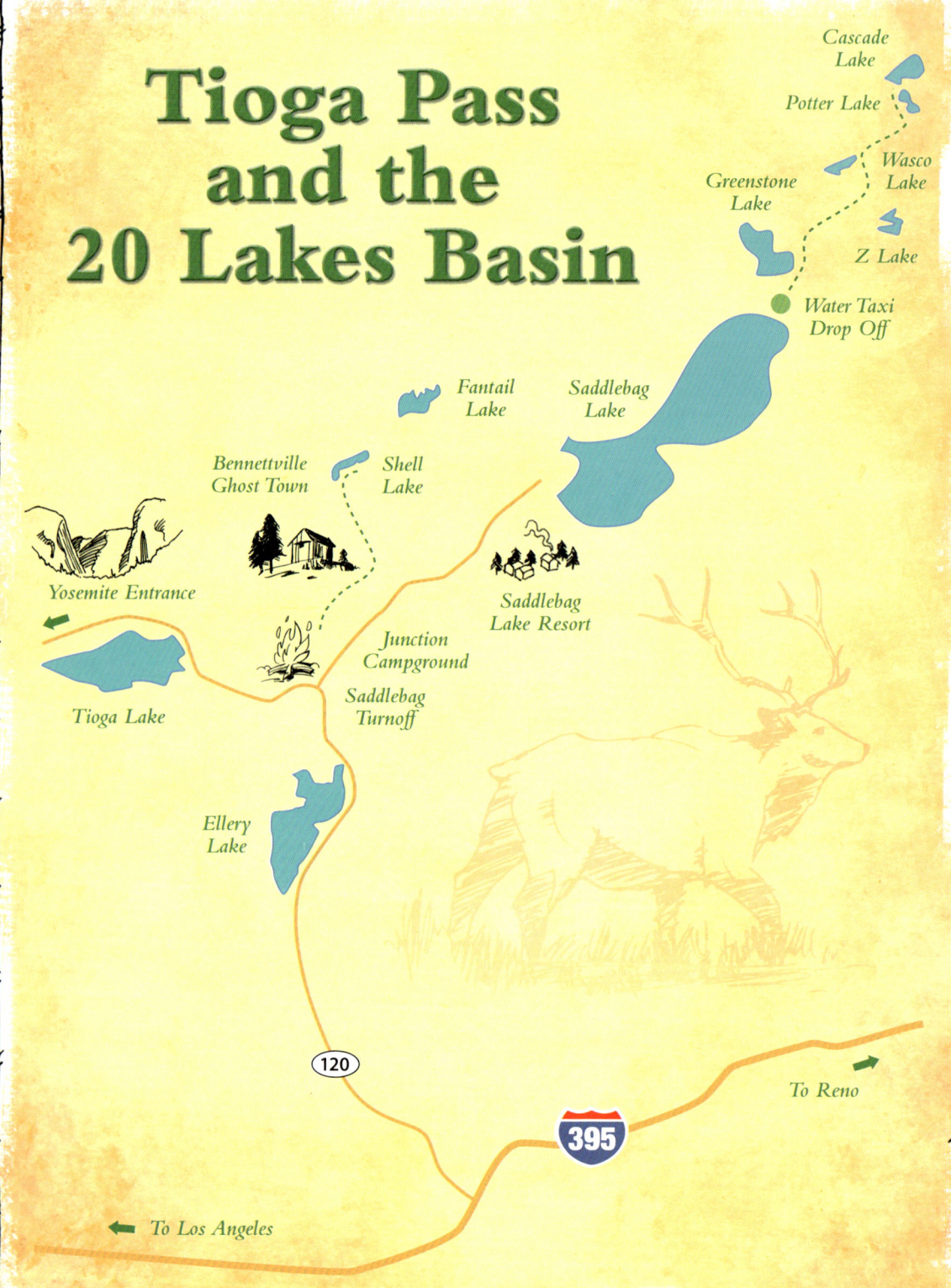

Trailhead: **20 Lakes Basin / Saddlebag Lake**
Elevation: **10,131 feet**
Climb: **60 feet**
Distance: **0.25 miles**
Lake Size: **23 surface acres**
Species: **Brook & Rainbow Trout**

Chapter One:
Greenstone Lake

Alright, folks, I'm going to level with you; this isn't really a hike. It's more of a short walk. In fact, there may be more walking involved in making it to the Saddlebag Lake store from the parking lot than there is to reach this backcountry lake. At a quarter of a mile, many of us walk farther around the grocery store every week. Still, there is a trail and this is a back-

Fishin' Trails

country lake so I wanted to include it in the book, if for no other reason than to show just how easy it can be to access waters that provide a taste of the backcountry experience.

From the water taxi drop-off point, you'll head up the trail to your left following the creek for five minutes or so until you reach the shores of Greenstone. That's right, five minutes, if that.

One of the largest lakes in the 20 Lakes Basin, Greenstone is especially beautiful with its strikingly bright turquoise water and Mt. Conness as a backdrop. When the sun's rays finally peek out from behind a cumulous cloud on a partly cloudy afternoon, the lake literally lights up, much to the onlooker's delight. Incredibly picturesque and completely accessible, that is what a trip to Greenstone is all about. Of course, anglers don't stop here just for the views, even if an argument could easily be made to do so. No, this lake also holds a population of wild Brook Trout that offer some action for those looking for their wild trout fix. From time to time, a Rainbow will make it into the lake, but that's quite rare.

While the lake holds mostly small fish under 9" in length, the ferocity with which these trout attack a fly or a lure makes Greenstone worth your time. There is little need for advice when it comes to techniques, as you're likely to catch plenty of fish with any assortment of flies, jigs, trout worms or small lures. One thing to note is that being a much larger lake, long casts will help you cover more water in less time so a casting bubble will prove helpful when fishing trout worms and flies.

The most important factor to consider when fishing Greenstone is location. The majority of the lake is extremely shallow so there is relatively little deep water. Most of this deeper water is towards the northeast side of the lake where the trail winds near the shore. In my experience the fish tend to stick to the deeper water or the area adjacent to it, so keep that in mind when fishing here. With most of the anglers and hikers continuing on up the trail to lakes above Greenstone, fishing pressure is usually light considering the lake's accessibility.

The last factor to account for when fishing Greenstone is the wind. The lake's size and location contribute to afternoon winds that often make fishing in the prime areas difficult if not downright unpleasant. Knowing that, you'll obviously want to schedule your fishing time as early in the day as possible.

So there you have it. Even though Greenstone is the shortest hike in this collection, there is certainly no shortage of wild trout or scenic vistas here.

Trailhead: **20 Lakes Basin / Saddlebag Lake**
Elevation: **10,310 feet**
Climb: **240 feet**

Distance: **1 mile**
Lake Size: **3 surface acres**
Species: **Brook Trout**

Chapter Two:
Wasco Lake

    From where the Saddlebag water taxi drops you off, Wasco is just one mile and 20 or so short minutes up the left trail. You'll climb a meager 240 vertical feet, most of which is accomplished in the first half mile. Even the best of us get winded when hiking above 10,000 feet but even so, this is a very easy hike. You'll pass the incredibly scenic Green-

Fishin' Trails

The Author's sister Lindsey Smith taking in the spectacular scenery at Wasco

stone Lake on your way there, as well as a few barren tarns that on calm mornings, offer incredible photographic opportunities as the towering Mount Conness and North Peak reflect off the surface of the water.

I suspect you'll be stopping plenty to snap photos of the incredible scenery on your way to Wasco. Don't forget to stop and look behind you once or twice as you're winding through the twisted juniper and stunted pines on your way up the hill. The view down on Saddlebag, Greenstone Lake, and the unnamed pond above is breathtaking! Just over half way to Wasco the trail straightens out, eventually taking a turn to the east at which point Wasco will be in clear view.

Unlike some of the other lakes in the area that hold Brook Trout topping out at 8", Wasco hides Brookies upwards of 10" for those willing to fish hard for them. Being a small, elongated lake, there is great access all the way up and down the eastern shoreline. Access on the western shore is also decent with exception to the sheer rock face that one has to contend with. Of course, with that sheer rock face comes deep water, so casting from either side is a good ploy. Aside from the area on either side of the rock face, I haven't noticed fish balling up anywhere specific but all the fish I've caught or seen caught there were out of deeper water. The middle section of

> "For plastics, it's impossible to beat the trout worm here. While having scented baits will get the fish to hold on a bit longer, color is everything here so come prepared with a decent variety of colors."

the lake offers your best access to the deep water from eastern shore.

Typically, you won't see any surface action at Wasco, nor are you likely to see any fish cruising the shallows. In fact, on my first trip there I thought the lake may have winter-killed at some point but as it was in my case, patience will bear fruit here, so stick with it.

Wasco has larger Brook Trout than most of the lakes in the basin

In most of the surrounding lakes, spinners and spoons work well but I haven't had much success using them at Wasco. Having said that, Rebel does make a small grasshopper/cricket lure that can work well for those who are intent on fishing lures. Now that's not to say that spinners will never work here; they just haven't worked for me.

Flies and plastics on the other hand have produced and have done so consistently. Wet flies and small streamers fished with the fly/bubble rig are a great choice for Wasco and provide the added advantage of being able to cast virtually all the way across the lake. Purple or olive woolly buggers with some flashabou will get the job done, as will your standard nymph patterns. Let the fly sink down for a few seconds after casting to get your offering down in the water column; and then start with a slow, jerk-jerk-stop retrieve. If you don't get any love with that retrieve, accelerate your retrieve or try a slow, less erratic retrieve.

For plastics, it's impossible to beat the trout worm here. While having scented baits will get the fish to hold on a bit longer, color is everything here so come prepared with a decent variety of colors. Unlike most lakes where Brookies are the prevalent species, orange is not necessarily the hottest color at Wasco. Truth be told, I've never even been bit on an orange trout worm here. For me, the best colors have been pink, red and white in that order. The fish at Wasco seem to prefer a very slow retrieve allowing the bait to bounce along the bottom and, in some cases, strikes will come while the worm is sitting idle.

Trailhead: **20 Lakes Basin / Saddlebag Lake**
Elevation: **10,300 feet**
Climb: **240 feet**

Distance: **1.4 miles**
Lake Size: **3 surface acres**
Species: **Brook Trout**

Chapter Three:
Potter Lake

    Fifteen minutes or so of mild hiking beyond Wasco Lake will get you to Potter Lake. From Wasco, you'll hike past two small tarns at which point you'll want to keep an eye out for a small trail that veers off to your left. Once on that trail you will cross a small gully before heading up and over a rise to the west. Continue on to the northwest and before you know it, you'll reach the boulder-dotted shores of Potter Lake. If you stay on the main trail you'll end up at Steelhead Lake but that isn't where you're trying to go, so if you arrive there, you passed the turnoff. Getting to this lake can be a real challenge early in the season with all of the snowdrifts present. Take that into account when planning a visit here. Also use caution when crossing any snow banks; I assure you that doing a face plant into wet melting snow is much more entertaining in those Warren Miller ski films than it is when it happens to you.

> "Despite its small size, it holds a prolific population of 5 to 8" self-sustaining Brook Trout."

Potter Lake is a very small body of water and could easily be characterized as a pond. Despite its small size, it holds a prolific population of 5 to 8" self-sustaining Brook Trout. These wild trout are game for just about anything you put in front of them, which is good news for us. The upper half of the lake is very shallow and while the Brookies will cruise that area, the best water is invariably the deeper pocket on the north side of the little island, even though that isn't a very deep spot either. Tossing a split-shotted fluorescent orange trout worm into that hole will produce plenty of fish. The usual assortment of flies, jigs and spinners will do the trick as well, but the little Brookies truly go gonzo for the trout worms.

The inlet is another productive spot as the fish are concentrated there and anyone tossing a fly can catch a seemingly endless number of the small Brookies. Just be careful not to back-cast one of the smaller model trout into the grass behind you!

Even with the solid fishing, my favorite thing about Potter Lake is the scenery. Boulders big and small are strewn about, abandoned by the glaciers that shaped them ages ago. The stunted waist-high evergreens and the majestic North Peak towering above make this my favorite spot in the basin to sit down and relax. Because it is off the main trail, it's also an excellent place to get a bit of solitude.

Trailhead: **20 Lakes Basin / Saddlebag Lake**
Elevation: **10,320 feet**
Climb: **260 feet**

Distance: **1.5 miles**
Lake Size: **8.22 surface acres**
Species: **Brook & Brown Trout**

Chapter Four:
Cascade Lake

    Cascade Lake and Potter Lake connect to each other with a tiny stretch of Mill Creek and the two are literally only a few yards from each other. If you find your way to Potter, you might as well check out Cascade because you're pretty much already there. Cascade Lake is a tremendous place to spend an afternoon as the fishing, scenery and the likelihood that you'll have the lake to yourself are as good as it gets in the basin.

The Brook trout in Cascade are slightly larger than those at Potter Lake and the quantity of fish is remarkable. You can start fishing just north of the outlet and work your way up the east shore. The first point north of the outlet is a good spot because it offers access to both shallow and deep water. Tossing lures is a sound choice here; silver Kastmasters or spinners in silver or gold should get bit.

> "Although that statement is true for all of the lakes in this book, a camera is just as critical as a fishing rod on a visit to Cascade - it's that gorgeous!"

The second point up the east shore is another spot that deserves a few casts as there is a steep drop-off there; in fact, you're pretty much standing atop what would be a sheer cliff if the lake was empty. Next as you work your way up the shoreline you'll come to a spot where you can cast into a little cove and that's where you'll want to break out your 1/64 ounce tube jigs and a bobber. Rig the jig 4' to 7' under the bobber and cast out along the cliff. Slowly working the jig along the rock face is like dynamite. For whatever the reason, the fish seem to ball up in that little cove and cruise around in a small school.

The last area that begs mentioning is the northwest corner of the lake. I recall a trip during the summer of 2005 where my sister, Lindsey, and I both caught 20 plus fish from this spot in just over an hour and a half. I was tossing a pink and white 1/64 ounce tube jig 4' under a bobber and she was pitching a size 0 gold Mepps spinner. There is a beautiful stretch of stream flowing down through the flats above the lake and it's loaded with fish. Unlike the fish in the lake though, the fish in the creek are very easily spooked, so use tact when approaching them. A few other spots along the west shore invite your hook and line: where the water comes cascading down the rock face of North Peak above; and the sizeable inlet at the southwest corner of the lake. These are all great places to fish.

DO NOT forget your camera on this trip. Although that statement is true for all of the lakes in this book, a camera is just as critical as a fishing rod on a visit to Cascade – it's that gorgeous!

Trailhead: **20 Lakes Basin / Saddlebag Lake**
Elevation: **10,440 feet**
Climb: **375 feet**

Distance: **1 mile**
Lake Size: **3.7 surface acres**
Species: **Brook Trout**

Chapter Five:
Z Lake

    To reach Z Lake you'll go up the left trail from the water-taxi drop off near the inlet of Saddlebag Lake and wind your way up the hill towards Wasco Lake. Just short of Wasco Lake, where the trail makes a turn west, you'll need to break away from the trail and hike cross country. In addition to the trail's obvious turn towards Wasco, a seasonal stream crossing the trail marks the spot where you need to break off and hike cross country to the northeast. It's easiest to follow the creek channel up for about 30 yards before turning to the east. You should come to a tarn shortly after leaving the trail and Z Lake is just a short jaunt beyond that.

A fun idea, for when you make your plans to visit Z Lake, is to spice up your day by making your visit part of an ultra short loop trip. Starting at Saddlebag, you can hike up to Greenstone, Wasco, then to Z Lake and finally end up at Hummingbird before heading back down to Saddlebag to nail a few planters while waiting for your water taxi. The whole hike is just over two miles and will allow you to see a lot more country than if you were to simply hike to and from any of those lakes.

Z Lake rocks, plain and simple! It's off the beaten path and absolutely loaded with 7 to 9" Brook Trout, two traits visiting anglers certainly can appreciate. In addition to its isolated location and the volume of fish waiting for you, this lake is astoundingly beautiful with photo opportunities literally in every direction. The water is crystal clear and shimmers a bright blue-green in the afternoon sun. The peculiar shape of the lake provides a regular playground for these trout and tends to channel them into the various finger-like areas.

There is no secret to catching fish at Z Lake. In fact, making your way there is where the lion's share of the effort lies. It is worth mentioning though that these fish go bonkers for orange or red trout worms and jigs, and the brighter the color the better. Work the baits slow from the deeper stretches all the way to shore. You'll be surprised by how many bites you'll have within only a few yards of the bank. Bring along your fly box and bubbles on this trip as well. I've had the best luck with wet flies like nymphs and tiny streamers fished behind a long leader. If you're a lure tosser, my advice is to stick with spinners. The fish here seem to really like chasing the sparkling blades of a small Panther Martin or Mepps. As with fishing plastics at Z Lake, I've watched fish chase a lure for 30 feet before finally mustering up the will to bite the lure so don't give up on a cast until the lure is literally at your feet.

For the photography enthusiasts out there, don't forget to hike around the south shore of the lake where a gorgeous tarn lays set behind the lake. There is a perfect opportunity to catch Mt. Conness reflecting off this stunning little pond.

Visiting and fishing a trout-filled lake for which there is no trail is a special feeling, one that is usually reserved for backpackers. Z Lake gives one the opportunity to experience that feeling in only a few hours time.

Trailhead: **Shell Lake Trail / Junction Campground**
Elevation: **9,850 feet**
Climb: **200 feet**

Distance: **1.5 miles**
Lake Size: **4 surface acres**
Species: **Brook Trout**

Chapter Six:
Shell Lake & Bennettville

    Of the lakes in this book, Shell Lake's inclusion was the only one based more on the trip to the lake than what you'll find at the lake. That's not to say that you won't find yourself with an opportunity to catch plenty of wild Brook Trout, but the area has much more to offer than just fishing. Fellas, if your best gal doesn't care much for fishing, this would be a great hike to take her along on because the hike is easy, the scenery is phenomenal and the historic relics are fascinating.

You can catch the trail to Shell Lake near camp site number One at the Junction campground at the Saddlebag Lake turnoff. One of the easier hikes in the book, the incline is mellow and the hike pleasant.

The first stretch of the hike is relatively uneventful, however, just prior to reaching the half mile mark, things get interesting. Two wooden structures come into view, which is surprising, considering you're in the backcountry. If you take the time to hike over to them you'll find two buildings: A small, one-room, single-story cabin of sorts and another, much larger, two story building. Wooden windows and doors offer a chance to get a great look at what's inside of these almost ancient structures. It is next to impossible to keep your mind bridled while walking around in these structures, as inevitably you find yourself imagining what it must have been like more than 100 years ago when they were built.

All that is left of the town of Bennettville

After my first trip to the area I was compelled to do a little research in order to learn what the deal was with this place since I'd never heard of it before. After a few impromptu interviews with some experts and plenty of surfing on the Net, I found what I needed to satisfy my curiosity, well, for the most part at least. I learned that the mine is referred to as the Great Sierra Tunnel, while the old wagon road, now used as a trail to access the area from the south, was once called the Great Sierra Wagon Road. The two wooden buildings are all that's left of what once was a thriving town known as Bennettville. These buildings date back to the late 1800s. Apparently a lost lode of silver is what initially brought folks to this spot, a lode of silver that to this day has not been found. It's still impressive, however,

Fishin' Trails

The Mine at Bennettville

to think that over a hundred years ago the old miners were able to bore nearly 2,000 feet into the mountainside, even if it was all for naught. With the mine bearing no fruit, or silver as it were, the financial backers of the venture called it quits and the mining activity ceased almost as quickly as it started. A ghost town with a touch of mystery on the way to a lake full of Brook Trout — how cool is that?! So, as you'll understand after your first trip to Shell, the allure of this place goes well beyond a fishing opportunity. It's also a chance to admire, even touch, our history. It is crucial that when visiting this historic place that you tread lightly and respect the structures for the treasures that they are.

If you stay on the trail past the buildings you'll come to a creek. To head to the lake you continue on the trail that follows the creek, but I would suggest crossing the creek and following the trail to the west a short ways to the site where the old mine was. A gaping hole blasted out of mountain, the remains of rails used for mining carts and some old rusty mining equipment including an ancient compressor are evidence enough of the work that was done there. The tunnel goes so deep into the mountain that it accumulates and channels the groundwater into quite a stream that pours out of the mine shaft and trickles down to the meadow below to join Mine Creek. I must tell you folks, it is quite a sight.

It should be noted that while visitors can walk a short ways into the mine tunnel itself, which, by the way, is very cool, there is a steel barrier intended to keep people from going in too far. Why, you ask? It's because the oxygen levels decrease as you make your way down into the mine. One could easily fall victim to the bad air and pass out, even die, so unless you're hip to becoming a permanent part of this heritage site, you'd be well served to respect the barrier that is in place and leave the rest to your imagination. A United States

Forest Service employee, who will remain nameless, told me that if people continue to break through the barriers put up by the USFS, they will blast the mine entrance to permanently close it. Needless to say, it would be a travesty if it came to that. If by chance you come across some jackass trying to pry their way through the barrier, resist the temptation to shake them violently like a rag doll, but do please take the time to educate them.

The old stable at Bennettville

Once you're done checking out Bennettville and the old mine, head back to the creek crossing and take the main trail north along the creek. Shell Lake is only a quarter mile or so past the old buildings. It's certainly an interesting lake and a scenic one as well. To get a mental picture of the underwater topography of this lake, imagine that winding its way through an elongated meadow is a deep streambed that one day got a little too big for its britches and overflowed its banks. That pretty much sums it up.

The fish in this lake are predictable so you'll want to stick to the inlet, the outlet and the deep channel that winds its way through the lake. The west shore offers good access to the majority of the deeper water but there are some good spots along the eastern shore as well. The scenic value of the lake, especially from the inlet, is phenomenal with the unmistakable Mt. Dana accenting your view to the Southeast.

As far as techniques go, this is your standard small Brookie lake, so you're going to score best with small jigs, flies and trout worms, but you're liable to catch fish no matter what you use. The fish near the inlet are especially fond of nymphs, regardless of the time of season or time of day. You're not likely to find any fish over 9" in Shell but you'll still have a ball and find that Shell is definitely worth the trip.

Trailhead: **Junction Campground / Tioga Pass Area**
Elevation: **9,900 feet**
Climb: **250 feet**

Distance: **2 miles**
Lake Size: **8.61 surface acres**
Species: **Brook Trout**

Chapter Seven:
Fantail Lake

    Fantail is about a half mile past Shell Lake on the same trail. With only 50 feet or so in elevation gain between Shell and Fantail, it is an extremely easy hike. The ease of the hike paired with the out of this world scenery make it well worth the effort. Although this is one of the longest hikes in this collection at just over two miles, the easy access, tremendous scenic value, and wide open fishing compelled me to include it in this book. As if the mild nature of the hiking isn't enough, the hike from the inlet of Shell all the way to the outlet of Fantail is alongside a creek stuffed full of Brookies, so if you get a hankerin' to fish along the way, by all means, do! Also, in between Shell and Fantail is a small pond that, while shallow, is also full of trout.

Fantail Lake is brimming with Brook Trout in the 5 to 9" range with the average being about 6". For the most part, the lake is shallow, giving it a unique look as the lake takes on a golden hue under the rays of the sun. Much larger than Shell, below, you can still fish your way around this lake inside of an hour without any difficulty.

Fish can be found just about anywhere around the lake, but there are three spots which I find especially productive. First are the inlets, especially the main inlet coming in from the West. The fish stack up here like you wouldn't believe, in fact, with favorable skies and some polarized sunglasses you can see hundreds of fish waiting for an easy meal to be swept down into the lake. Unlike most wild trout, these fish are not particularly spooky so you can afford to be bit less cautious than you normally would have to be at a backcountry lake.

Early in the season there are several smaller inlets that are also productive. Another great area is around the islands. You can cast to these islands from either side of the lake but I find the best access is from the west shore, just north of the inlet. Casting a pheasant tail, hare's ear or prince nymph at this spot will produce a lot of strikes. The last notable spot is along the eastern shore where the winding creek channel has bored into the lake bottom close to shore. The water is deepest here, which makes this a good spot mid-day.

The fish at Fantail are anything but picky so regardless of skill level, anglers should expect to get some action. My best success has been when using split-shotted wet flies or 1/64 ounce tube jigs, but I think it's more about personal preference than technique at this particular lake.

It should be noted that a gorgeous stretch of creek winds through the tundra-like meadow above the lake. I've personally witnessed and photographed more than 30 fish in a single pool in this remarkable area. Easy access and tons of fish translate into excellent fishing, especially for those with the urge to cast a dry fly!

Virginia Lakes Basin

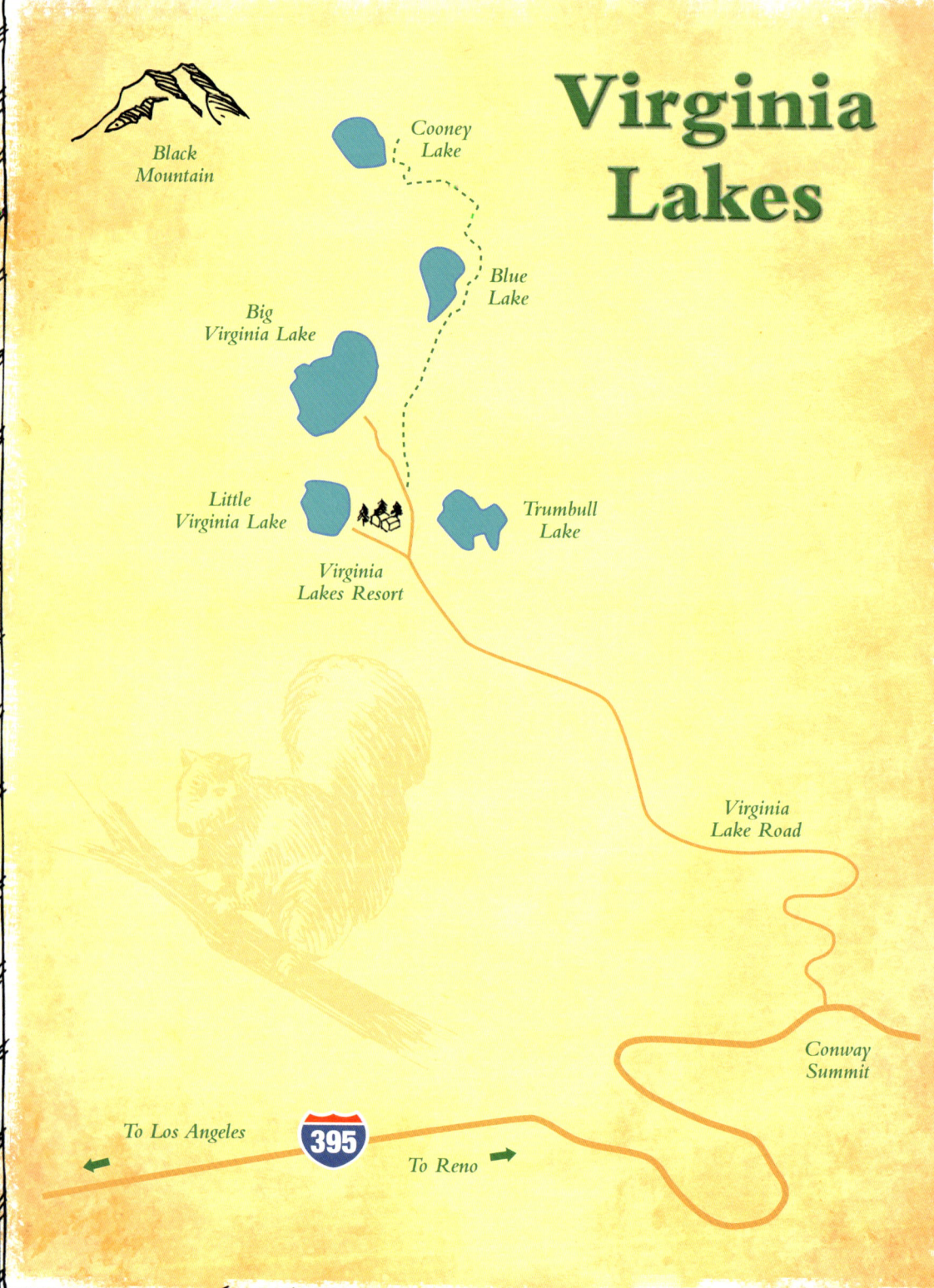

Trailhead: **Big Virginia Lake**
Elevation: **9,888 feet**
Climb: **80 feet**

Distance: **0.40 miles**
Lake Size: **9.3 surface acres**
Species: **Brook, Brown & Rainbow Trout**

Chapter One:
Blue Lake

The word "hike" barely applies to the jaunt to Blue Lake from the parking lot at Big Virginia Lake. It would be better characterized as a mellow stroll through the forest. Easy and short, two of my favorite descriptors when it comes to hiking, can describe this hike. Although it only takes 20 minutes at the very most, views of the creek and the dense forest

Fishin' Trails

make taking your time a necessity. There's no rush up here, folks, so slow down and enjoy yourself; that's part of what makes hiking special!

Blue Lake has dense populations of wild Rainbow and Brook trout that will keep just about anyone highly entertained for a few hours, if not the whole day. Location makes a big difference when fishing this lake so you'll want to concentrate your efforts towards the inlet and outlet for the best results. Early in the season, a few small, snow-fed inlets add some interest and opportunity to the main inlet coming down from the lake above. These inlets bring food into the lake, concentrating the fish and making it easier for anglers like you and me to score big numbers of trout on visits to Blue.

A great spot to fish early in the afternoon is the point on the north side of the lake just before the willow-spotted bank turns to shale. A few summers back while researching for this book, my good friend Mike Rigney managed to land nine Brookies and two Rainbows from 5 to 10" at this spot in less than 30 minutes of fishing. I don't care who you are, that's fun! While you may not see results like this every time you visit, it would not be a surprise if one managed 50 fish or more in a good day's fishing at Blue Lake. Another nice thing about this gem is that the vast majority of the hikers seen in the area don't bother fishing at Blue…go figure. As if the great fishing and easy access to this lake wasn't enough reason to entice a visit, the scenery is nothing short of phenomenal. Blue Lake is an example of just how good it can get just a few short minutes from a trailhead.

As far as tackle goes, there isn't necessarily a bad way to fish this lake. In my experience, everything from flies to spinners will produce. Having said that, there are a few techniques that prove deadly here and will help you catch more fish than if you randomly pulled items from your tackle box to try.

First and foremost are trout worms. The Brookies and 'Bows in this lake go absolutely bonkers for bright orange trout worms, so that's a great place to start. Split-shotting the trout worms is probably the easiest way to rig up but the water bubble rig will allow for longer casts and that's a good thing here. Flies are also top producers at Blue, especially near the main inlet where a well presented female Adams or Elk Hair Caddis will often be ferociously attacked by a wild trout only seconds after hitting the water. Green or white tube jigs fished under a bobber and a variety of small Panther Martins or Mepps spinners are also favorites.

Trailhead: **Big Virginia Lake**
Elevation: **10,249 feet**
Climb: **450 feet**

Distance: **1.25 mile**
Lake Size: **9 surface acres**
Species: **Brook & Rainbow Trout**

Chapter Two:
Cooney Lake

To reach Cooney you'll start at Big Virginia and make the leisurely hike that takes you by Blue Lake, after which you begin to climb and gain elevation. The trail along Blue is well marked but please, do watch your step on the stretch that crosses the large shale section, to avoid taking a spill on those sharp rocks. I can tell you from experience that it hurts.

Fishin' Trails

> "At well over 10,000 feet, the alpine landscape is breathtaking and the striking blue-green water, impressive. I recommend you start fishing right where the trail first meets the lake."

Watching your step might seem like a very simple thing to do but with the exceptional view down on Blue Lake, it's easier said than done, I assure you. I wouldn't consider this hike to be strenuous per say, but it certainly will get the blood pumping. Of course that is generally true anytime you're hiking at over 10,000 feet of elevation. Take your time, folks; the lake will still be there when you arrive.

My favorite part of this hike is a small ancient looking log cabin that you'll come across about half way to Cooney. The weathered old wood structure sags to one side, which adds to its charm. It's quite a sight. Some crudely assembled wooden tables and the remains of a bed frame, among other debris, occupy the cabin's interior.

It's fun to look around, but be forewarned, the cabin isn't particularly stable so it's best viewed from outside through the door or one of the windows. If you allow your mind to wander a bit, you'll find there's something about that little cabin that conjures up colorful visions of the Old West. It's a great place to take a break from the hike, catch your breath, have a snack and snap a few pictures.

When you arrive at Cooney you'll know immediately it was worth the sweat you expended to get there. At well over 10,000 feet, the alpine landscape is breathtaking and the striking blue-green water, impressive. I recommend you start fishing right where the trail first meets the lake. A few casts with a size one gold Mepps is almost sure

The Old Cabin up the trail from Blue Lake

to entice a healthy 7 to 10" 'Bow or Brookie to strike.

As you survey the lake, note the point on the north side of the lake because it's a great spot. On the far side of that point is the main inlet. The creek comes in and branches off. What's left are a few patches of land providing superb access to the countless trout waiting for dinner to

Cascading inlet to Cooney

float down into the lake. Although the lake fishes well just about all the way around, you'll want to focus on the inlet, the deep water near the very obvious cliff face and around the back side of the lake near the rock slide. In addition to the main inlet, a small inlet on the far side of the cliffs is worth a shot, too.

The fish in Cooney are relatively easy to fool so whatever style of fishing you prefer should produce at least a few fish. Brookies and 'Bows to 13" are here but the majority of fish will hover around 10". Trout worms are definitely worth your time at Cooney, especially where water enters the lake. In my experience, red and orange are the most reliable colors but I'd bring along other colors as well just to be safe. Small Panther Martins, Kastmasters and Mepps

are the lures of choice. Flies, of course, are also productive. Working a split-shotted wooly bugger or nymph near the inlet is a sure bet to score some fish, too. In July of 2005 my mother, Judy, caught the most beautiful brook trout I've ever seen using that very setup. It was such a gorgeous fish that it ended up on the cover of this book.

A beautiful wild Brook Trout

Angler's Slang

Anglers have their own set of slang words and being that I'm an avid Angler, I think, talk, and inevitably write using some of these terms. For those of you who may not be hip to some of the terms I use in this book, I've included this short list as a cheat sheet.

Bendo – When you have that beautiful bend in your rod caused by a fish pulling at the end of your line.

'Bow – Rainbow Trout

Brookie – Brook Trout

Brownie – Brown Trout

Bubble rig – A clear casting bubble is completely filled with water, secured 4' to 7' above the worm and held in place with a swivel or Carolina Keeper.

Cutts – Cutthroat Trout

Drop-shot rig – Attaching a Palomar Knot to a thin wire hook, then attaching a split shot sinker to the tag end of the knot. Vary the distance of the bait from the bottom by adjusting the length of the tag end.

Farm a fish – Getting bit but missing the fish.

Fishing Pressure – The amount of use a given body of water gets. For instance, places like Crowley Lake see thousands of fishermen each season and thus experience heavy fishing pressure.

Flashabou – A metallic material used in fly tying that gives flies like Wooly Buggers a bit of flash so they stand out.

Hatches – When insect larvae transition to being adult bugs, it is said that they hatch. It is during these times that fishing with flies is stellar.

Planters or Stockers – Hatchery-raised Rainbow trout that the Department of Fish and Game stocks in most of the roadside lakes and streams in the area. They're fun, but far less desirable than wild Trout.

Skunked – Getting skunked means you're not catching any fish; it's the big goose egg, zero, zilch. You often hear anglers say things like "I've got to get the skunk off."

Split-shot – Uses a thin wire hook on which the worm is threaded (or wacky-rigged) with a small split-shot sinker attached 12 to 24" above the worm

Tarn – A small pond; the term is often used by backcountry folk.

Trophy Fishing – Fishing with the sole purpose of catching a huge trout.

Contact us to inquire and to order additional copies of

Fishin' Trails:
25 Short Hikes for
Eastern Sierra Wild Trout

Fishin' Trails
c/o Parchers Resort
5001 South Lake Road
Bishop, CA 93514

Enjoy more photos of the spectacular Eastern Sierra at:

www.EasternSierraAngler.com
www.EmerickPub.com
www.SmithSierraPhotography.com

To purchase prints of any of the photographs taken by the author for this book, please visit www.SmithSierraPhotography.com.